A Baseball Career That Ended in . . .

A Split Second

Keep the faith

jim Aldridge

A Baseball Career That Ended in . . .

A Split Second

The Life and Faith of Jim Aldredge

JERRY GUIBOR

iUniverse LLC
Bloomington

A BASEBALL CAREER THAT ENDED IN . . .
A Split Second
THE LIFE AND FAITH OF JIM ALDREDGE

iUniverse books may be ordered through booksellers or by contacting:

iUniverse LLC
1663 Liberty Drive
Bloomington, IN 47403
www.iuniverse.com
1-800-Authors (1-800-288-4677)

ISBN: 978-1-4917-0167-6 (sc)
ISBN: 978-1-4917-0168-3 (ebk)

Library of Congress Control Number: 2013914079

Printed in the United States of America

iUniverse rev. date: 08/10/2013

Contents

PART THREE

The Halls of Learning

PART FOUR

The Career Years

PART FIVE

The Years at City Hall

PART SIX

The World of Education

PART SEVEN

A Legacy

Trust in the Lord with all your heart and lean not on your own understanding; in all your ways acknowledge him, and he will make your paths straight.

—Proverbs 3:5-6

The Lord is my shepherd, I shall not be in want. He makes me lie down in green pastures, he leads me beside quiet waters, he restores my soul. He guides me in paths of righteousness for his name's sake. Even though I walk through the valley of the shadow of death, I will fear no evil, for you are with me; your rod and your staff, they comfort me. You prepare a table before me in the presence of my enemies. You anoint my head with oil; my cup overflows. Surely goodness and love will follow me all the days of my life, and I will dwell in the house of the LORD forever.

—Psalm 23

In that old rugged cross, stained with blood so divine,
A wondrous beauty I see,
For 'twas on that old cross Jesus suffered and died,
To pardon and sanctify me.

—verse three, The Old Rugged Cross

Give thanks to the LORD, for he is good; his love endures forever.

—1 Chronicles 16:34

Train a child in the way he should go, and when he is old he will not turn from it.

—Proverbs 22:6

Prologue

Upon examination, a baseball exudes a charm that is deceptively soft and maddeningly hard. It's a siren clothed in cowhide . . . with an alluring sweet spot.

What is this thing, a baseball, which seemingly takes on a personality of its own? It comes in one size, 9 inches in circumference, and one weight, 5¼ ounces, at most, light enough to be thrown 100 m.p.h. and heavy enough to travel more than 500 feet on the fly.

It even has been said that some batter somewhere knocked the cover off the ball, though nobody has ever seen that happen in an official game.

Under those two stitched-together leather covers, ever so close to the surface, is cotton yarn, which gives way to wool yarn and then tougher wool yarn, but if the cover does come off, when sullied and battered and torn, string is all over the place, miles of it, before the rubber-covered cork center appears for a second, then bounces wildly down the street.

Baseballs come from a factory where they are seemingly stuffed, between all that yarn, with line drives, bleeders, towering home runs, bad hops and errant throws, causing all description of joys and insults. Those taut threads, all 108 stitches, can leave angry imprints on an ankle or shin or arm or worse, looking like a red tattoo, dispensed capriciously, much like life itself. There is no explaining any of it, but why did the ball turn on one of its own? Why did it find Jim Aldredge and his promising career in the Pittsburgh Pirates' organization come to a halt, just like that, all too soon, in a split second?

There are no answers, only the question: He can still play, can't he? They tell him he can, and he's game for one more chance—even if it means interrupting his education, his all-important insurance against life's ups and down, even if it means one or two more minor league towns, and more political and racial indignities. Especially because he's only 19 years old and he could hit a baseball as easily as breathing and chase down that siren in the outfield as swiftly as the best could.

Introduction

There is no doubt that Jim Aldredge was a top prospect, and the encomiums and bon mots roll off the tongue easily about him, almost too easily. After all, he last played in 1963, and memories play tricks on us after that many years ago. The stories grow into legends and improve with age, and soon they are masquerading as the gospel. Baseball people swear by them.

At the time, Bob Fontaine, one of the two Pirate scouts who signed him, said Aldredge could be the next Roberto Clemente. The other scout, Don Lindeberg, didn't go quite that far, but there is always a manager who tags a young player as a "can't-miss." In spring training, longtime manager Sparky Anderson was always saying such-and-such a player would become the "next Mickey Mantle," and that player was doomed, snakebit, and probably didn't even make Anderson's team.

Today, scouts and baseball people testify that Aldredge "could really hit the ball." Or: "He could chase down long fly balls with the best of them." Or: "He was destined to have a big league career." Or: "He was a five-tool player." Even though that description didn't exist in 1956 when Aldredge signed.

So, how good was Aldredge?

Taking into account the unabashed writing style of sportswriters in 1955, which looks as quaint as one of them reporting in a news story "our Fresno Grizzlies" in the 21st century, let the record and some box scores tell the tale as Aldredge progressed through his high school years to spring training to his two years as a professional baseball player:

HIGH SCHOOL

McClatchy News Service reported:

> *The Madera High School baseball squad won its first Yosemite League contest in three years here [Madera] yesterday afternoon when it downed the Edison High Tiger nine, 9 to 8, in an extra inning game.*

Later in the same story:

> *Aldredge led the Edison hitting with two home runs in the third and fourth innings. He was also the mainstay in the Tiger fielding with several near impossible catches in center field.*

* * *

After the final Northern Yosemite League baseball game of the 1956 season, McClatchy Newspapers Service wrote:

> *The Edison High School Tigers of Fresno, depending on the big bat of James Aldredge and the steady pitching of Walter Jones, defeated the Merced Bears, 11 to 5.*

> *Aldredge blasted two home runs. His first came in the seven run fourth inning, 388 feet into centerfield. His second round tripper cleared the left centerfield wall at 400 feet and is believed to be the longest ball ever hit by a prep player in Merced's Civic Ball Park.*

* * *

Late in 1956, a Fresno Bee headline and story announced:

> *Stars Sign Aldredge*
> *For Bonus of $4,000*

Pittsburgh Pirate scouts Bob Fontaine and Don Lindeberg signed Aldredge, and Lindeberg was quoted in the news story:

> *"We will take Aldredge to training with us next spring and he will have every chance to make the team. We think he has tremendous possibilities and we were very happy to sign him. We have watched him for several years and I know a lot of teams were interested in him."*
>
> *Aldredge batted .417 for Coach Mickey Mansini's Edison team last season and walloped nine home runs.*

*　　*　　*

Another Bee headline and story:

> *Fresno Baseball School*
> *Stars Whip Sacramento*

Fresno Bee sportswriter Bruce Farris observed:

> *Aldredge, the youngest player on the field at 15 years, was a stickout in all departments and coaches on both clubs predicted a fine future for the Edison High School junior.*
> *The big speedster smashed a double and a single in four trips, drove in one run, scored another and made two sparkling running catches in center field.*

*　　*　　*

In the baseball school's playoffs in 1955, the Fresno Bee headline:

> *Aldredge Homer Leads*
> *Fresno All Star Club To*
> *9-4 Win Over Modesto*

Writing from the Modesto press box, Bee sportswriter Farris started the game dispatch thusly:

> *James Aldredge walloped a tremendous home run to ignite a five run eighth inning rally and give The Fresno Bee, KMJ, KMJ-TV All Stars a 9 to 4 baseball victory over the Modesto Bee KBEE All Stars before 1,000 fans in Del Webb Field last night.*

*   *   *

In the championship game of 1955, the Sacramento Bee, KFBK All Stars thumped the Fresno Bee, KMJ, KMJ-TV, All Stars, 7-4. In the game story, sportswriter Farris noted:

> *Aldredge, who at 16 years old, has another year of school competition left, again sparkled at bat and in the field . . . His rifle throws brought much applause as did his two fine running catches.*

1957 SPRING TRAINING

Fresno Bee headline:

> *Jim Aldredge Hammers*
> *Five Hits for Hollywood*

The lead paragraphs in The Associated Press account:

> *James Aldredge, 18 year old outfielder on the Hollywood Stars and a former Edison High of Fresno diamond star, had the biggest day of his professional career yesterday when he collected five singles and stole two bases in Hollywood's 9 to 5 exhibition victory over the San Diego Padres.*

> *Aldredge was signed by the Stars and is expected to be optioned to the San Jose JoSox of the California League. He is making a strong bid to stay with the Stars.*

Hollywd	AB	H	O	A	S. Diego	AB	H	O	A
Christpher, rf	5	3	3	0	Robinson,cf	4	1	2	0
Smith,ss	5	0	2	3	Moran,ss	4	0	4	3
Toothmn,2b	5	2	2	0	Lockln,lf,1b	5	2	8	0
Pettit, 1b	3	1	6	0	Regalado,3b	2	2	1	1
Minice, 1b	0	0	0	0	Metkvich,1b	3	3	2	1
Goss, cf	5	1	4	0	Grant, rf, p	5	1	2	0
Aldredge, lf	5	5	2	0	Young,2b	3	0	0	2
Baumer, 3b	4	1	0	2	Jones, c	2	0	3	0
Hall, c	4	0	4	0	Thomas, p	2	0	1	0
Wade, p	0	0	0	0	Grace, ph,c	2	0	3	0
Mtemyor, ph	0	0	0	0	Kazak, 3b	1	0	1	0
Hayson, p	0	0	0	0	Rapp, lf	2	0	0	0
Bernier, ph	1	0	0	0	Murszski,p	1	1	0	0
Raydon, p	2	0	0	0	Davidson, rf	1	0	0	0
Koback, c	1	0	4	0					
Totals	**40**	**13**	**27**	**6**	**Totals**	**37**	**10**	**27**	**8**

Montemayor walked for Wade in 4th.
Grace flied out for Jones in 5th.
Bernier grounded out for Hayson in 6th.
Davidson flied out for Murszewski in 8th.

Hollywood 013	100	400	-- 9	13 1
San Diego 200	030	000	-- 5	10 2

1 -- Robinson, Daumer, Kazak. SB -- Aldredge 2. RBI -- Regalado 2, Aldredge 2. Toothman, Christopher 4, Metkovich, Grant 2, Goss, Baumer. SF -- Baumer. 2b -- Toothman, Baumer. 3B -- Grant, Goss. HR -- Regalado, Christoper. DP -- Smith-Pettit. LOB -- Hollywod 11, San Diego 10. BB -- Thomas 3, Haysom 1, Murszewski 3, Raydon 3. SO -- Thomas 3, Wade 1, Haysom 1, Raydon 4, Grant 2. H -- Off Thomas 8 in 5, Wade 5 in 3, Haysom 3 in 2, Murszewski 5 in 3, Grant 9 in 1, Raydon 2 in 4. R-ER -- Thomas 5-4, Wade 2-2, Haysom 3-3, Murszewski 4-4, Raydon 0-0. HBP -- Regalado (by Wade). Winner -- Raydon. Loser -- Murszewski. U -- Kerr and Mutart. T -- 2:37.

CALIFORNIA LEAGUE

In 1957, the San Jose JoSox edged the Fresno Sunsox 4-2, and Ed Orman reporting for The Fresno Bee wrote:

> *In the ninth Jim Aldredge, rookie centerfielder from Fresno, drilled a single through the infield into center. The former Edison High School star stole second and third baseman Jim Campbell's singled pushed him to third after first baseman Dick Minice whiffed. Whitman grounded to shortstop Bob Geels. It was a double play ball but Geels chose to try to stop Aldredge at home. He made an inept throw in front of catcher Nat LeBlanc and Aldredge was already in.*

From the same report:

> *Aldredge also made a sensational catch of [Gary] Rushing's drive against the wall at the 400-foot mark.*

* * *

The United Press reported about San Jose's 6-1 win over Visalia in San Jose and said Aldredge doubled twice and singled to drive in three runs for the JoSox.

Visalia	AB	H	O	A	San Jose	AB	H	O	A
Pirela, ss	4	2	3	1	Figuroa,2b	4	2	3	3
Pinson, rf	3	1	4	1	Dgherty,ss	5	2	0	3
Castillo, 2b	4	0	0	0	Aldredge,cf	4	3	1	0
Gaines, lf	4	0	1	0	Hutzler, rf	4	1	2	0
Stack, 1b	3	0	7	0	Whitman,lf	1	0	0	0
Kennedy,c	4	0	6	0	Campbll, 3b	4	1	3	5
Bivens, 3b	3	1	0	3	Minice, 1b	3	0	12	0
DeMartini,cf	4	1	2	0	Brown, c	4	0	5	0
Dunn, p	2	0	1	1	Perry, p	4	2	0	0
Edwards, ph	1	0	0	0	Wright, lf	3	0	1	0
Moreno, p	0	0	0	0					
Totals	32	5	24	7	Totals	36	1	27	11

Edwards hit into force for Dunn in eighth.
Visalia . . . . 000 000 010 -- 1
San Jose . . . . 040 000 02x -- 6
R - Campbell, Minice, Pery, Figueroa 2, Aldredge, Bivens. E -- Dougherty, Campbell, Stack. RBI -- Perry, Figueroa, Aldredge 3, Hutzler, Pirela. 2BH -- Aldredge. 3BH -- Hutzler. LOB -- Visalia 7, San Jose 11. BB -- Dunn 8. SO -- Dunn 4. Moreno 1,Perry 5. H&R --Dunn 8 for 4 runs in 7 innings. Moreno 3 for 2 runs in 1. ER -- Dunn4, Moreno 2, Perry 1. HP --Figueroa (Dunn), Whitman (Dunn), Pinson (Perry). WP --Perry 2, Dunn. W -- Perry (11-). L -- Dunn (11-5). U -- Mc-Kinney and Shimada. A -- 923. T -- 2:09.

WESTERN LEAGUE

The Lincoln Evening Journal headline:

> *Aldredge Homer in 4th Gives*
> *Chiefs 2-1 Win Over Demons*

Reporter Don Bryant wrote:

> *Leave it to the Lincoln Chiefs and the Des Moines Bruins[1] to provide first class baseball action.*

> *The two Western League clubs did it again Friday night, with the Chiefs taking a 2-1 victory on the strength of Jim Aldredge's two-run home run and a eight hit pitching job by lefty Al Jackson.*

> *Lincoln got only four hits off two Demon pitchers, and Aldredge got two of those. But his fourth inning homer was enough to give Lincoln the series win, 2-1, and keep the Chiefs on top of the league.*

DES MOINES	ab	r	h	bi	LINCOLN	ab	r	h	bi
Coombs, cf	4	0	1	0	Javier, 2b	3	0	1	0
Holdfield,rf	4	0	1	0	Looney, 1b	4	0	0	0
Hartsfield,2b	1	1	1	0	Plaskett,3b	3	0	0	0
Parker, 2b	4	0	1	0	Aldredge,lf	4	1	2	2
LeJohn,3b	3	0	1	0	Washngton,rf	1	0	0	0
Lindsey, lf	2	0	0	1	Sada, ss	2	0	0	0
Asprmnte,ss	4	0	1	0	Cigar, cf	2	0	0	0
Kohorst, c	4	0	0	0	Piver, c	3	0	1	0
Wendt, p	2	0	0	0	Jackson, p	2	0	0	0
Smith, p	1	0	1	0					
a-Sickel	1	0	0	0					
Totals	33	1	8	1	Totals	24	2	4	2

a -- Struck out for Smith in 9th.

Des Moines . . . . 100 000 000 -- 1
Lincoln . . . . 000 200 00x -- 2

E -- Sada. PO-A -- Des Moines 24-14; Lincoln 27-14. DP -- LeJohn-Parker and Given; Parker-Aspromonte and Given; Sada-Javier and Looney; Javier and Looney. LOB -- Des Moines 8, Lincoln 5.

HR -- Aldredge.

	ip	h	r	er	b	so
Wendt (L, 0-1)	4	3	2	2	6	1
Smith	4	1	0	0	1	7
Jackson (W, 1-1)	9	8	1	1	2	8

HBP -- Jackson (LeJohn). PB -- Piver. U -- Haack and Hergert. T -- 2:19. A --804.

---

[1]   Des Moines' nickname was the Demons. Who were the Bruins? It is an editing mystery to this day.

*   *   *

Before we enter the Life and Faith of Jim Aldredge, there is one more anecdote. After Aldredge signed with the Pirates, a St. Louis Cardinal scout told him the next spring that they would have signed him for $100,000, making him a Bonus Baby.

The Pirates made lefty Paul Pettit the first Bonus Baby when they signed him for $100,000 in 1950. Pettit won exactly one major league game before he developed a sore arm. Would the Pirates have taken another gamble? Probably not. Indeed, there were no bidding wars. So, would the Cardinals have really made such an offer? No one will ever know.

Certainly, there is a long list of Bonus Babies who failed. Of course, Sandy Koufax was the grand success story; he was the exception. Joey Amalfitano was the mild success story. To be sure, money doesn't guarantee success, especially not in baseball.

*   *   *

Nevertheless, there are two more testimonies. Consider them valid.

Fresno Temple Church of Christ Pastor Harry Miller remembers how Jim was "one of the best baseball players in the city of Fresno and the Valley before he graduated from Edison, although he probably won't tell you anything about this."

Kalem Barserian, the president of American Dried Fruit, who played on teams with Aldredge, said: "Not only would Jim have been the next Willie Mays, without question, if he had not suffered the eye injury playing minor league ball, but he is one of the most honorable men that I have ever met. In fact, if I could be someone else in life, it would be Jim Aldredge. That's how special a man he is."

PART ONE

The Baseball Years

Chapter One

April 23, 1958

When Jim Aldredge came out of the clubhouse to warm up that night, the Lincoln Chiefs were opening a home stand against the Amarillo Gold Sox. They had just returned home from a two-week road trip to Topeka and Albuquerque.

Now, it was time to play catch and only natural that he sought out Tony Washington, one of his roommates in spring training.

"Hey, Roomie," Aldredge said, "who they throwing tonight?"

"Don't know who he is," Washington replied. "All I know is he's a right-hander."

"Well, that means I'm hitting third, and you're right behind me, hitting fourth."

Aldredge batted third when facing a right-hander, and Washington, a left-handed batter, fourth. Manager Monty Basgall flip-flopped the two in the batting order when a left-hander was pitching. It was his best attempt at making his lineup more productive.

"Know what he throws?" Aldredge asked.

"Don't know that either. But I know you can hit him."

*   *   *

It was encouraging news because Aldredge had gotten off to a slow start. It was too early in the season to call it a slump, but he was hitting a disappointing .245 in 28 games for the Chiefs of the Class A Western League.

In his rookie season with the San Jose JoSox, he batted .284 and led the California League in triples with 15, hitting with power mostly to right-centerfield. Impressive, but not everything the Pirate organization expected out of a player 6 feet tall and 195 pounds, and strong. The Pirates wanted him to pull the ball and generate more home runs. As a result, he was topping the ball to the left side of the infield.

*   *   *

Aldredge had begun his second season of professional baseball in Lincoln, so he was somewhat familiar with the ballpark, but a mental review of the friendly confines of Sherman Field seemed like a good idea. Little did he know it was the last time he would see the place as a player.

The grass had been mown earlier that day and was the limpid green of a pristine spring, and Aldredge took in the fragrance and basked in the moment.

Home plate was in the northwest corner, and the sun was starting to slip below the rim of the wooden roof covering the grandstand, and he wouldn't be looking directly into it by game time. The lights hadn't yet taken hold, or had they? After all, it was a Class A minor league park, and the lights were just adequate.

The ballpark was a wooden structure, rustic looking, and the wood fences were strangely void of any advertising for that era. The proprietors of Armstrong Furniture and Allen's-Alley, which called itself "the fishing headquarters for South Lincoln," chose to advertise only in the game program, which cost 10 cents and included a smiling photo of manager Basgall.

The layout was symmetrical, 345 feet down each foul line and 405 feet to straight-away center field. The dugouts were just that—dug out and a dirt floor, and players had to walk down narrow, cramped steps. In the clubhouse, players hung their street clothes on hooks. There were no lockers. The shower room gave the whole place the smell of a musty gymnasium.

Aldredge noticed a slight breeze wafting from left field across to right, carrying the aromas of cigar smoke and popcorn to the far reaches of the park. But it wasn't strong enough to drastically alter the flight of a fly ball, and certainly not when Dick Stuart hit 66 smoking home runs two seasons earlier.[2]

---

[2]   Stuart smashed 66 home runs for Lincoln club of the Class A Western League in 1956; the total is one of the highest in the history of baseball.

Sherman Field held a few thousand fans but, more than likely, there were fewer than 1,000 present that night. The team's average attendance that season was 463 friendly Nebraskans. It's impossible to say whether they knew there was a young phenom named Aldredge in their midst. They hadn't seen him play for Edison High School in Fresno or seen his dazzling performance in a Southern California Winter League game just before he signed.

Chapter Two

"CAN'T-MISS"

Baseball talent scouts started to take notice when Aldredge was 15, and, a year later, when he hit two home runs in one game at Merced, they knew he had power and could run. The first left the park towering far above the 388-foot mark; the second was an exciting inside-the-park sprint.

In June 1956, Aldredge was graduated from Edison High School in Fresno. He had turned 17 on May 1, and he was busy working in the fields, starting summer classes at Fresno City College and squeezing in time to play in a twilight baseball league.

While the St. Louis Cardinals were doing everything possible to sign him and send him east to the Triple A International League, the Pirates had an ace up their sleeve that the Cardinals couldn't trump. The Pirates enticed him with an even more alluring contract, knowing Aldredge wanted to stay near his mother in Fresno. They simply promised Aldredge he would begin in the Pacific Coast League[3] with their affiliate, the Hollywood Stars. (Had it been one year earlier, Aldredge indeed may have become a Cardinal because the Cardinals still had a farm team in Fresno.) The only other enticement the Cardinals could offer was a beer distributorship.

If beginning a career one step away from the majors wasn't heady enough for a 17-year-old, the Pirates also lured him with his first plane ride and flew him to Los Angeles for a tryout in the Winter League. But his first plane ride was memorable for all the wrong reasons. The plane

---

[3]   The Pacific Coast League was designated an open classification, higher than Triple A, and was regarded by some as the "third major league." Some players supposedly refused a big league promotion because it would have meant taking a pay cut.

was a puddle-jumper. Aldredge's description says it all: "It seemed to hit one air pocket for every one of my 17 years on Earth. I prayed to God to grant me an 18th." He learned that a black man's knuckles could turn white.

As nerve-wracking as the flight was, the specter of facing top pitchers—professional and amateur—was still to come. Aldredge passed easily. At the plate, he went 2-for-5. In the field, he made a sterling running catch that took away an extra-base hit. It was mid-November 1956.

*   *   *

The Pirates needed no more convincing, and, two weeks later, they sent their top scout, Bob Fontaine, to wrap up the deal at Aldredge's ramshackle, sharecropper's house in west Fresno. It was a two bedroom, wood-framed shack that was unprotected by paint against the hot San Joaquin Valley sun. When it rained, the roof leaked. The toilet was out back. A lawn to mow? The yard was bald dirt.

Aldredge said, "At first when the scouts came around, it was embarrassing, but they were statesmen-like."

The date was set for Fontaine's visit, and all the arrangements were made. That's a polite way of saying, Aldredge's mother made certain that her alcoholic husband was out of the picture. He wouldn't be coming in roaring drunk and trying to run off somebody "who didn't belong in his house." And, oh Lordy, it was *his* house, wasn't it?

Mrs. Aldredge—all the scouts liked her and took to calling her Ida—was the perfect hostess and served cookies she had baked.

It was an overly simple arrangement. Aldredge was his own "agent," to use that term loosely. "Gee," he recalled, "I was only 17 years old." There was no bargaining—all of the other scouts were offering the same $4,000—but he had the presence of mind to say that he wanted to go to college. Aldredge had been contacted by Stanford University baseball coach Dutch Fehring. Such a grand plan was secondary because Aldredge needed the signing money. "I had to get my mother out of the marriage situation," he said.

While signing with the Pirates was a pragmatic dream come true for Aldredge, he would have preferred completing four years of college. He chose professional baseball first only for his mother's sake, and not many people realized that. "Earning enough money to finance my mother's divorce from my father took precedence over everything," he said, and he hid his true preference from his mother. He didn't want to hurt her feelings or make her feel guilty.

So, Fontaine offered—and Aldredge accepted—a $4,000 bonus and a $600-a-month salary, a lot of money back then. Aldredge didn't even bother to read the contract. "I trusted Fontaine," he said. The Pirates never mentioned college again.

The bonus left him just short of qualifying as a Bonus Baby. The Bonus Rule said that any bonus over $4,000 meant that the player must be on a major league team for two years. The Pirates wanted Aldredge to play immediately and not merely ride the bench in the big leagues the whole time.

The Pirates figured it was only a matter of time Aldredge would reach the majors anyway. They immediately tagged Aldredge as a "can't-miss" prospect. Fontaine went even further, declaring Aldredge the next Roberto Clemente, already on his way to a Hall of Fame career.

Using the signing money wisely, Aldredge bought a 1955 Buick and paid for his mother's way out of a difficult marriage.

Chapter Three

PLANS CHANGE

When spring 1957 came and it was time to go to his first training camp, Aldredge hitched a ride from Fresno to Los Angeles with a friend of the family who lived in Los Angeles. The friend dropped him off at the Greyhound station in the center of the city, and he took a bus to Anaheim, the site of the Hollywood Stars' training camp. He settled in at the Disneyland Hotel and moved about the hotel easily. No one hassled the young black ballplayer. After all, it was sunny Southern California, and exactly 10 years after Jackie Robinson broke baseball's color barrier and three years after the U.S. Supreme Court ruled against the separate but equal principle.[4] Nevertheless, major league teams weren't all that enlightened. It would take another two years for Pumpsie Green to become the first black player to break into the Boston Red Sox's lineup, the last team to accept integration. Still, racism remained in the blood of grizzled managers and coaches, and, in baseball's backwater towns and cities, Aldredge was in for a cold awakening.

During spring training games, Aldredge was playing against Green and others he considered his baseball heroes—Monte Irvin of the New York Giants; former Dodger World Series hero Joe Black; Cleveland Indian pitcher Jim "Mudcat" Grant; pitcher Earl Wilson in the Red Sox's farm system[5]; outfielder Carlos Bernier, pitcher Ben Wade and slugger Dick Stuart, all owned by the Pirates; and another slugger, Steve Bilko,

---

[4]   The milestone case was Brown v. Board of Education of Topeka, Kansas.

[5]   Wilson was promoted to Boston in July 1959, one week after Pumpsie Green. They were the first African-American players signed by the Red Sox.

with the Los Angeles Angels. The biggest thrill of all was a game against the Red Sox and seeing the outfield of the great Ted Williams, Albie Pearson and Jim Piersall.

With those stars in his eyes and Bob Fontaine's promise of making the Stars' opening-day roster on his mind, Aldredge was fully inspired to show everyone he could play at that level. He batted over .300 in spring training and played error-free in centerfield. In one game against the San Diego Padres, the Cleveland Indians' top farm team, he went 5-for-5 and stole two bases.

His accomplishments were all the more noteworthy because he had other worries circling in his mind. Was the judge's restraining order really enough to keep his wayward father away from his mother?

As he learned later, everything was fine at home, but the mysteries of baseball politics made his head swim when the Pirates changed plans. Despite an excellent spring, Aldredge was dropped all the way to San Jose in the Class C California League, considered the lower minors. Class D was the bottom. The Pirates bypassed the A and AA levels, all the while assuring Aldredge his talents were considerable and emphasizing there was no need to rush his development.

Naturally, Aldredge felt betrayed by the Pirates—but intact were his belief and faith in God, something instilled in him at his mother's side as her voice filled their house with spiritual songs and he witnessed her faithful prayer life.

He went to San Jose willingly, determined to overcome this "demotion." Once there, he realized he would play the entire season there because there was a full-length picture of him in the JoSox's game program. It also was an exercise in minor league economics. The team's budget most likely wouldn't have allowed new programs to be printed if he had been called up and a new photo inserted. More to the point, the Pirates obviously told manager Dick Whitman he would play every day. And play he did. He started every game for San Jose—all 140 games.

There were additional residual bonuses. The JoSox were scheduled to play three games against the Fresno Sun Sox and against the Visalia Redlegs, allowing him not only to visit his mother in the midst of her divorce but also to sleep in his own bed.

Chapter Four

"WHITES ONLY"

In 1958, major league baseball made its move to the West Coast, and the Brooklyn Dodgers were no more. The Dodgers took up residence in Los Angeles and the Hollywood Stars also became a footnote in baseball history and were moved to Salt Lake City. The team took "Bees" as its new nickname to satisfy Utahans and their Beehive state. The Pirates' top farm team also had its spring training camp moved to Jacksonville Beach, Florida.

Living conditions there were nothing like the genteel Disneyland Hotel in Anaheim. Black and Latino players were told they could live in a flophouse above a bar, and the music blared all night, every night. They took their meals at a greasy-spoon diner that was a plywood hut—no windows, no door, only square gaps in the wall. The ghetto's streets were paved with mud.

Racism was still entrenched in the South, and nobody cared about anybody's baseball pedigree. Consider these teammates of Aldredge's who were black: Donn Clendenon, who would star for the Amazin' Mets in the 1969 World Series; Al Jackson, who pitched for the Pirates and three other big league teams in a 10-year career; Al McBean, another Pirate pitcher; and catcher Elmo Plaskett as natural a hitter as there ever was.

Before a game in Daytona Beach, Aldredge carelessly forgot himself and sat down in the "Whites Only" section for a moment before he went into the clubhouse. He was still in his street clothes.

"You don't belong here," a white female usher informed him. "Go sit out there in the outfield bleachers. That's where you belong."

Incredulous, Aldredge said, "I am a player who is scheduled to play in today's game."

The woman silently turned and pointed to a sign: "No Colored People In This Section. Whites Only."

Just as silently, Aldredge prayed for restraint and strength to endure, and left for the clubhouse and prepared to face future Hall of Fame right-hander Bob Gibson.

Pitching in the sixth inning, Gibson was showing the dominance and grit that characterized his career. It has been said that he'd even drill his own mother in the ribs if she stood too close to the plate. And this was only a spring training game, for crying out loud. Gibson was working on a no-hitter when Aldredge came to bat for the third time. He swung through a fastball and then watched a curve veer wide outside. On the next pitch, Aldredge singled sharply into centerfield, spoiling the no-hitter.

As intense as ever, Gibson glared over at Aldredge on first base. Aldredge shrugged and these thoughts ran through his head: "I ain't mad at you, and it's nothing personal. It's simply that Jim Aldredge is not planning on going back to the cotton fields of west Fresno County."

He frankly didn't care how tough Gibson was, saying: "Once the ball left his hand, he no longer had control of the situation. I had control of the situation."

After the game, Aldredge allowed himself a moment of pride, satisfied that he was able to show restraint in a moment of racist tension and not let it upset his pregame preparation.

"You can persevere," Aldredge said, "if your faith in God is strong, and you have the willpower. Anything less than that and a black or Latino player couldn't make it because it's even more difficult when many of the fans in the city where you are playing don't necessarily want you around or even like you."

*   *   *

Such racism was not confined to the South, and Aldredge suffered similar humiliation at other stops where it was least expected—crackers in the South, sure, but in the West, too?—Brawley, California; Reno, Nevada; and the Tri-Cities area of Richland, Kennewick and Pasco, Washington. As a kid, he already had received similar abuse in Coalinga, Taft and Arvin, California.

While in Reno for a series against the Silver Sox, the JoSox's black players could not stay or eat meals at the team hotel. A dive motel was their only choice, and they took their meals at a combination bus station/casino. A woman dealing blackjack told them: "Even Mr. Johnny Mathis, the famous singer, is living in a motel, and not in the downtown hotel where he is performing nightly." The players protested to manager Dick Whitman, and the team moved to an integrated motel near the ballpark. The JoSox's white players backed the change.

* * *

Aldredge and his teammates were relieved when the 1958 spring training was over. When camp broke, Aldredge was promoted and reassigned to the Class A Lincoln Chiefs in the Western League.

Lincoln's manager, Monty Basgall, asked Aldredge to make a rookie from the Caribbean feel comfortable in his new surroundings. The rookie, Elmo Plaskett, and Aldredge, and three other teammates, were in for another shock.

The Chiefs had boarded the team bus in Lincoln and were headed for Albuquerque for a three-game series. In Dalhart, Texas, the bus rolled into a motel parking lot. The white players on the team filed off the bus and into the motel lobby.

As Aldredge, Plaskett, Al Jackson, Julian Javier and Tony Washington were about to step off the bus, Basgall told them they wouldn't be able to eat in the motel restaurant, but they could stay in rooms in the back of the motel.

"So," the manager said, "don't get off the bus just yet."

"At that moment," Aldredge said, "tears streamed from my eyes down my face for the first time since elementary school."

After waiting in the dark on the bus, they were finally directed to the back of a nearby restaurant where they were allowed to eat. Aldredge gave a large, but sarcastic, tip to the little old white waitress who served them. It was only then that they were shown to the rooms in the back of the motel where they stayed overnight on the way to Albuquerque.

Chapter Five

THE ACCIDENT

After the swing through New Mexico and Kansas, the Chiefs returned to Lincoln and were opening their second home stand, this time against the Amarillo Gold Sox.

Aldredge had popped up in his first appearance at the plate, but chopped a single between third and short in his second at-bat. The standing order from the Pittsburgh front office was for him to learn to pull the ball and hit for power. Aldredge was accustomed to hitting into the right-centerfield gap.

"It became a struggle," Aldredge recalled, "for me to try and pull the ball to the left side of the field, and my overall batting average was at first hampered. But, according to the wishes of the organization, I was learning how to pull the ball better to both our satisfaction and with power."

Next up was roommate Tony Washington, as swift a runner as Aldredge. Washington hit a hard bouncer to the right of the second baseman, Jerry Streeter[6], who later said he shouldn't have been anywhere near the ball. But he speared it and flipped the ball backhanded out of his glove to the shortstop, Clyde Perry. The ball arrived slow and low, and Aldredge was approaching like a tank. Perry snatched the ball off the top of the second base bag with his bare right hand and fired the ball, submarine style, toward first.

"I saw the ball as his arm came across second base, and he released it," Aldredge once told The Fresno Bee. "I tried to duck as I was sliding,

---

[6] Streeter, who coached baseball at Modesto Junior College from 1966-1982, was an assistant there in 2013 at age 81.

but it was too late. It all happened so fast. The ball struck me squarely in the left eye at point-blank range."[7]

Recalling the accident clearly 55 years later, Aldredge said: "It burst the eyeball like a grape."

The sound echoed throughout the ballpark, much like the crack when a bat meets a ball. As sweet as that sound is, the sound of the ball meeting Aldredge's eye was sickening. "Horrible," Streeter said in 2013. The sound was etched in his mind's ear.

---

[7]   Aldredge was quoted in a feature story in The Fresno Bee on Aug. 30, 1981, written by sportswriter Jan Peterson.

Chapter Six

"I'm Coming Home"

Somehow, Aldredge never lost consciousness on his way to the Lincoln hospital. All the while a melody began to run through his mind. "This thought resonated from one of my favorite religious hymns, 'Just Hold out Until Tomorrow and Everything Will Be Alright.'"

At the hospital, he was fully aware as doctors prepared to begin a frightening procedure.

Though serious damage had been done to Aldredge's eye, they hoped it could be minimized. First, they had to stop the bleeding and brought out a long needle—"four or five inches long," Aldredge said. They had to insert it into the eye to draw out blood and relieve the pressure inside the eye. Aldredge can still see the needle as it came close to his eye and, just as vividly, remembers the crunching, squishing sound it made going into the eye. Unfortunately, the internal bleeding did not stop right away.

Despite unimaginable pain, Aldredge finally went to sleep and awoke the next afternoon with sight in only his right eye. He could see enough to know a nurse walked into his room. His first words to her were: "Did we win?"

His manager, Basgall, teammates and the opposing manager, Eddie Bockman, stopped by to visit. The opposing shortstop who threw the ball never did.

After four days, Aldredge was released from the hospital. He visited Sherman Field one more time before the Pirates arranged his flight home. "I phoned my mother and told her I was coming home," Aldredge said. He told her only that he had gotten hit in the head. She met him at Fresno Air Terminal.

Concerned about their top prospect, the Pirates wanted Aldredge to see the best ophthalmologist in Los Angeles. With their Hollywood connections—crooner Bing Crosby was a minority owner—the Pirates had access to the finest.

Aldredge and his mother got into the '55 Buick and headed down Highway 99. With only one eye, Aldredge drove. First, it was up the tortuous Grapevine and over the Ridge Route and then down into the Los Angeles Basin to the appointment.

"When the doctor shined the light in my eye to examine it," Aldredge said, "he immediately said: 'It's gone.' I had some peripheral vision, but I lost that. All the sight was gone in about six or seven months."

Back in Fresno, Aldredge consulted with other eye doctors to find out if correction was possible, especially for depth perception. With only one good eye, depth perception is greatly reduced. The only answer was to wear sunglasses to prevent further damage from sunlight and to protect his good eye.

Chapter Seven

A New Beginning

His career was over, and the Pirates gave him his outright release. Then came a phone call that sent chills up his back. A baseball scout was on the line.

"I watched you play a lot in San Jose," said Lloyd Christopher, a scout for the Kansas City Athletics, "and I really liked the way you play the game. I understand that you had an eye injury, but have you thought about coming back?"

In the midst of telling the story, Aldredge could not resist grinning from ear to ear. Of course he thought about it. He was playing some sandlot baseball.

"How are you playing?" Christopher asked.

"OK," Aldredge answered, "but not too frequently." He was working full time and taking classes at Fresno City College.

Christopher then proposed a tryout because he was convinced Aldredge with one eye had more talent, hustle, smarts and inner resolve than many ballplayers with two good eyes. Two weeks later, he took batting practice and worked out in the outfield at Fink-White Playground in west Fresno.

After the workout, the scout was more convinced than ever and signed Aldredge to a Triple A contract with the Kansas City Athletics. He would report to the Portland Beavers in the Pacific Coast League for the 1959 season. Christopher said, "If you make the team, you stay. If not, they have a minor league system where you can play at the level of your current talent and performance."

It was like the dawn of a new day for Aldredge, two months shy of his 19th birthday. He reported to spring training in Brawley in February, and more racial prejudice was waiting. After a seven-hour bus ride, Aldredge took a taxi to the team hotel. Pitching coach Larry Jansen intercepted him in the lobby and rushed him to the parking lot out back.

Jansen told him: "Jim, you will be living at the home of Mr. and Mrs. Calloway, which is just south of town. Two of your fellow ballplayers, Chico Valentine and Norman Bass[8], will be living in the next block with a private family also. All three of you will be living about one mile from the ballpark."

Aldredge said: "It's 1959, in California, yet here we go again with racial discrimination. Back in Fresno, I was in the process of earning a college education. Do I really need this aggravation?"

When Aldredge and Jansen arrived at the Calloways' house, in the heart of the city's barrio, Jansen told him he would have a home-cooked breakfast, then walk to the ballpark and suit up. He would expect to see them at 9 a.m. each day.

Aldredge, Bass and Valentine, a Panamanian, agreed not to yield to bitterness. Together, they said there were two options: Be bitter and quit, or be better and play. They vowed to be on Portland's roster when the team headed north to Oregon.

* * *

Again, Aldredge gave it his best shot, batting over .300 and making two plays that wowed even manager Tommy Heath, a cigar-chomping veteran. Aldredge charged in from center and caught a popup nobody seemed to want. He tumbled over second base at the end of the play. He also tracked down a drive straight over his head, at the 400-foot mark.

Aldredge's first reward was a baseball card contract worth $25 with Bazooka Bubble Gum Company and an equipment contract with Rawlings Sporting Goods Company. He used some of that Bazooka money and bought Norman Vincent Peale's best-selling book, "How to Live 365 Days a Year."

In the vein of positive thinking, he had molded this philosophy: "Hitting is a skill, speed is often an attitude, and defensive excellence is hustle and desire." He believed in showing "hustle marks" and doing the unrequired extras whether in sports or in any job in life.

---

[8]   Bass, a right-handed pitcher, was from Vallejo and the brother of former Los Angeles Rams running back Dick Bass.

His second reward was the best news: He had made the team.

*   *   *

His stellar play and desire led Heath to defy Kansas City general manager George Selkirk three times. Selkirk wanted to send Aldredge to the team's Florida training camp, for reassignment. Heath put his job on the line for Aldredge.

In the opening series at San Diego, Aldredge pinch-hit and fouled off two pitches before coaxing a walk. It was enough to convince him: "Man, I can play at this level."

His confidence was lifted even higher when the team played the Phoenix Giants, and he was on the same field as veteran Wayne Terwilliger, future superstar Willie McCovey and infielder Jose Pagan. He remembered: "I had every reason to feel I belonged."

As he was leaving Fresno, he said, "If I made it to the big leagues, I would be blessed. I told myself: I can do this because with God all things are possible if you believe."

It appeared the impossible—starting in centerfield—was about to happen when a teammate suffered a minor injury. It was game two of the Phoenix series, and Larry Jansen told Aldredge that the Athletics had traded for outfielder Russ Snyder and would join the team for game three. Jansen, the dutiful lieutenant, then gave Aldredge an ominous message. It's never good news when a player hears, "Go see the skipper."

Aldredge said, "When I arrived in the clubhouse, Tommy told me that since I was the youngest guy on the team at 19, he had to send me to another Athletics' farm team." Heath said he had done everything he could, but the politics of baseball had struck again. Sending a player down or releasing a player is the manager's toughest job.

"This time," Aldredge said, "I could not keep tears from coming down my face, having my spirit broken again by baseball. Just minutes earlier, my heart had been pounding because I had made it. I had made it. I was just one step away from the big time, 'The Show.' "

Heath tried to comfort Aldredge with these words: "I wish you could have stayed because you would have played a lot for me."

Jansen came in, asked for his uniform and told him to shower and watch the game from the stands.

Chapter Eight

HUMILIATION

Three days later, his assignment came, and he was sent to Sioux City, Iowa, to the Class B Three I League. In his first at-bat, he homered and went 2-for-4 as a replacement for an injured outfielder. When the player was healthy, Aldredge's job was pinch-hitting, pinch-running and platooning in left field with his roommate, John Cunningham. The competitive tension grew between them until it was unbearable. Conversation between them ceased.

The only way out was to request to be sent to another team in the Athletics' organization, and Aldredge was sent to the Tri-City Braves in Kennewick, Washington. He stepped back into the cesspool of racism and was not able to rent an apartment in Kennewick or Richland. He found a seedy motel in nearby Pasco. The clientele, inside and outside the motel, were transients.

Without a car, Aldredge was picked up by manager Jack "Lucky" Lohrke every day, and they rode to the ballpark until something else could be arranged. Everything about the situation was discouraging and embarrassing. After a 10-day road trip to Oregon, Aldredge told Lohrke he was going to take a bus to Fresno and return with his car. But he knew it was time to call it quits at age 19.

Aldredge said, "I think deep down inside I knew I would only need a one-way ticket to Fresno. I then decided to voluntarily retire from baseball and return to Fresno to resume my college studies."

Lohrke even had to deliver him to the bus station. "I felt a huge weight lifted from my shoulders when I got out of manager Lohrke's car at the Greyhound Bus station with all my belongings to head for Fresno." To make the situation even more humiliating—and laughable, the bus station was closed, and Aldredge sat awake on a bench all through the night, keeping an eye on his suitcase so he wouldn't be picked clean by the bums.

When the bus station opened, Aldredge bought a $30 ticket to Fresno, leaving him with 5 bucks, not even enough money to take a taxi to his mother's house. Fortunately, an acquaintance from the playground saw him walking near the bus station and gave him a ride home.

Next, he sent a letter of resignation from professional baseball to the Tri-City team and requested his final paycheck.

Chapter Nine

ONE LAST TRY

Working for the City of Fresno and back studying at Fresno City College, he was on track to graduate from Fresno State College by 1964. There was not a chance he was going to fritter away his life by hanging out at the local park with his buddies who thought they could be just like him and go from high school directly into pro baseball.

"Jim would have none of that kind of talk," the Rev. Harry Miller, a longtime friend, said. "He told many of us to get our education first because education was a commodity. Once we achieved it, no one could take it away from us. Jim always says that the level of educational achievement is a personal choice based on your desire and ability."

* * *

Nearly three years had gone by since he voluntarily retired from baseball when the phone rang one day.

"Hey, Jim, this is Ray Perry. Remember me from the California League? I understand that you went to Portland, and things didn't quite work out. Why don't you come over to Salinas to a New York Mets' tryout camp, and try out for us?" They had played against each other, and now Perry was a scout.

Another chance? Another workout? Another comeback? At age 22? The offer was like a dream that kept repeating itself. Aldredge had to do it. He had to be certain. He couldn't reject it with the wave of a hand.

After four days of impressive workouts, Aldredge had an epiphany, and he had one of those inner chats: "You've got to be absolutely kidding. You alone cannot navigate this major turning point in your life and in your faith without seeking God's wisdom and direction for your life."

He prayed all night until sunrise and said this message came to him, straight from his heart: "Jim, are you crazy? What if some guy hits you in your good eye? Then you'll be blind." That day, he thanked Perry and told him he had decided to go home and continue his education.

Again back in Fresno, Aldredge knew the burning desire to play baseball was quenched.

PART TWO

The Early Years

Chapter Ten

WAR TIME

James Earl Aldredge was born on May 1, 1939, to Lonnie and Ida B. Aldredge, in Gilmer, Texas, at that time a racially segregated town of fewer than 1,000 residents in East Texas.

Lonnie was a talented auto mechanic and carpenter, and Ida had homemaking skills that she learned from her mother. She also knew agriculture, which is a roundabout way of saying she had labored in the fields picking cotton.

A bright child who was a capable teacher's aide at the two-room schoolhouse, Ida wanted to go to college, but to continue meant she would have to finish high school in Tyler, 41 miles away, and live with relatives. Her mother forbade it because Ida was the oldest and needed to take care of her six siblings. Ida's schooling ended after the ninth grade.

After World War II began, news about California and the shipyards and "The Promised Land" came filtering through relatives back to rural Gilmer. Ida was the driving force in the family, and she saw an opportunity to improve the family and, of course, escape the oppressive Jim Crow laws of the South: separate but equal restrooms, segregated restaurants, separate drinking fountains for blacks, and all the other belittling prejudices.

When Aldredge was 4 years old, in 1943, the family, including older brother John, picked up and moved west to Richmond, California, and Lonnie and Ida started working at Mare Island Naval Shipyard. Because of the war effort, demand for civilian workers was great—regardless of their gender and skills and education and, most telling, the color of their skin.

*   *   *

The Aldredges found a room to rent in a house owned by Mrs. Almeda McGowan. For a little more than two years, all four of the Aldredges were crammed into the one-room addition at the back of her house in North Richmond. As a luxury, they had kitchen privileges—which went beyond just using the stove and ice box—and bathroom privileges in the main part of the house.

The elderly Miss McGowan, a kind and understanding woman, taught Ida Aldredge about urban living: how to use the telephone and the gas stove, and how to use the city bus. They were as close as family while waiting for the war to get over.

MISS ALMEDA McGOWAN

The kindhearted Miss McGowan was one of four people instrumental in imparting invaluable life lessons in the education of young Jim Aldredge. Ask children who their first teacher was and they usually give the name of the sweet lady in kindergarten or the first grade. Their first real teachers—their parents—often do not occur to them immediately. "Well, they aren't *real* teachers." Of course they are, and Aldredge had plenty of early instruction from his mother and father—even if the latter was negative—and Miss McGowan. The other three were *real* teachers, and they blossomed Aldredge as a pupil and athlete. You will come to them one by one.

Miss McGowan cared for Aldredge and his brother as if they were her sons. They were always welcome at the kitchen table and were honored even before Miss McGowan's guests.

Aldredge said, "She never stared at me and my brother or said, 'Get out of here.' None of that. Traditionally, black preachers from Baptist churches go to some church member's home and eat dinner. She did not let the deacons or preachers go to the table unless my brother and I were there. She'd say, 'Come on, John and Jim.' She never deprived us of anything. John was in the second grade, and I was in kindergarten."

On occasion, if the Aldredges' friends or relatives came from Stockton or from Texas to visit, she would make room for John and Jim in her bedroom. She was just like an understanding grandmother, in addition to being a tutor and mentor to Ida.

But Miss McGowan also worked, and Ida had to find a baby-sitter because she and Lonnie often worked overtime or double shifts to earn a living. The arrangement lasted only until Ida learned that the baby-sitter's son was bullying her boys and the baby-sitter had punished the boys by making them sit for hours in their chairs so the house wouldn't get messy. After that, Jim, 4, and John, 6, also had to watch out for each other. A year later, each day they went to San Pablo Elementary School. Half-day sessions were not uncommon in those days of wartime classroom shortages, and they were home alone from 1 o'clock until 4.

Neither Jim nor his brother John could tell time accurately, but they both knew what the long hand and the short hand of the clock meant.

When they heard Mrs. Aldredge open the creaking screen door and it slapped against the house, it was their happiest time of the day. Mr. Aldredge would usually come in around 6.

But then August 1945 came, the war was over and work slacked off as shipyards began laying off workers who lacked seniority or skilled trades. First, Ida lost her job, and, two weeks later, Lonnie was out of work. Because North Richmond was a rough area and because Ida had heard about the cotton fields of the San Joaquin Valley, she decided to move the family to Fresno.

The Aldredge family kept in touch for a while with Miss McGowan, but Jim Aldredge never saw her again. He missed her very much. Mrs. McGowan stayed in Richmond for another six months and then moved to Los Angeles to be close to her family. Aldredge said, "I planned on many occasions to go to visit Mrs. McGowan in Los Angeles, which was just 210 miles south of Fresno, and express my appreciation to her for what she had done for my family when we arrived in Richmond." He never did before she died. It's a regret that lives with him to this day. He shakes his head sadly while saying, "Mrs. McGowan's memory serves as a prime example of how you cannot deviate from your core principles without consequences." He said it taught him to always take care of unfinished business. Since then, Aldredge makes a point of helping people just as Mrs. McGowan helped him and his family.

Chapter Eleven

LESSONS OF RACISM

At first, Fresno was far less a "Promised Land" than Richmond. Certainly, Aldredge's father found a job at the Santa Fe Railroad warehouse using the trade he learned in the shipyards, and Ida found jobs doing housework.

She had to travel across town from where they were living—in a substandard migrant camp, later condemned—at Church and Railroad avenues in Calwa. While it was 1946, there was plenty of leftover evidence of the Great Depression. Indeed, they were living in a postwar Grapes of Wrath. Their tent "house" had a floor; other tents had only dirt floors. They drew water from a central faucet, and used outdoor toilets. Later, they came across an old, ragged house trailer, and Aldredge's father patched it together to make it livable.

The same year, Calwa Elementary School was integrated, but racism didn't magically end. Aldredge was in the first grade and John in the third. The only black kids at school, the Aldredge boys met racism face to face, and they had to fight their way home every day. There were fistfights with classmates and older pupils who called them names like "Sambo" and unashamedly screamed "nigger" at them. On their homeward retreat, they protected themselves by throwing rocks at their tormenters. The conflicts ended when word got around how tough the Aldredge brothers were—not to mention that the principal intervened.

Aldredge said, many years later, "I don't like to say it, but the school was comprised of a whole bunch of Southern whites living in that small community." It hurt him to learn that there were people who simply didn't like black people. It was a quick study in life at a young age.

*   *   *

The lesson was driven home again years later when Mrs. Aldredge took Jim and John by train to Gilmer from Fresno to visit a sick relative. Reaching San Angelo, Texas, the Aldredges had to wait for a connecting train and were suffering in the humidity through an 11-hour layover in a detached waiting room. One light bulb was barely enough to see the sign on the wall, but it clearly told the terrible story: "Colored/Negroes."

A kindly African-American custodian named Mr. White offered to take them to his house for the rest of the layover.

"My house is far safer than this train station waiting room," he said.

Mrs. Aldredge wasn't jumping at a strange man's offer.

"My wife and I have welcomed Negro travelers there before," he said. "Especially women with children. You shouldn't be sleeping any length of time in this station. It's a bad part of town, and it's dangerous."

Mrs. Aldredge first had to be convinced his wife was a Christian. When he said she was, and quickly added he was, too, she agreed.

Having finally settled in with their relatives in Gilmer, John and Jim walked into a local drug store and closer to the flame. Why they even ventured inside is beyond imagination. Their three cousins warned them: "None of you had better go inside."

At the soda fountain, John sat down to order his favorite ice cream cone.

"Hey, yooo," the lady behind the counter said in one of those cranky, high-pitched voices, "you can't sit there. If you want some ice cream, go around the back of the store to the window for the coloreds."

John was beginning to get real scared.

Unfamiliar with all the ins and outs of unwritten—but real—Jim Crow laws, next it was Jim Aldredge's turn for a stark lesson. At the local movie house, John and their cousins bought tickets first. Jim was last in line to approach the white woman inside the ticket booth.

He was 10 years old but big for his age. Of course, he could get in on an under-12 ticket. And that's when the heat started to rise.

The ticket booth lady proceeded to bait Jim by saying, "Boy, you must be going to be a giant when you reach 16."

"I guess so." Though polite enough, it was not the answer she wanted to hear.

A male usher standing close by said: "Hey, boy, you need to go back to the lady selling the tickets and say, 'Yes, ma'am,' to her."

Once he obeyed, he could go through the door that led to the stairway up the outside of the building to the balcony section that the whites named "The Crow's Nest" because only black people sat there. In fact, it was the only place they could sit. There was a portable concession stand tended by a black person.

The movie?

"I had no clue what the movie was about because I was so scared all through it," Aldredge recalled.

"However, 30 years later while on another family illness-related trip to Texas, you better believe that I made sure to visit that same drug store and was served from the counter. Conversely, my brother John, who died in 1983, refused to return to any place in the South at any time for the rest of his life."

Chapter Twelve

SCRAPING BY

Back home in Fresno, the Aldredges had scraped together enough money to put down a small amount on a rickety house on part of 10 acres of a sharecropper plot. The family's share was 3⅓ acres. Mr. Aldredge contributed only a small amount because his paycheck from Santa Fe rarely made it home.

He had started to drink, and he would booze away rent and food money. Any work that he did as a "jack of all trades" never amounted to anything because he sought to please his friends—all the while neglecting his family. His "friends" exploited him by seldom paying him.

Aldredge looks back and says, "He'd always have somebody's car to work on, or help to build a house. I can go show you three houses he helped to build and those guys never paid him a dime for any of them. All they had to say was, 'Man, you did a good job,' and that was it." Or they said, "I'll pay you later," and he would give an aw-shucks reply: "That's OK. It wasn't a hard job."

Then, the father's job came to an end when Santa Fe moved their warehouse operations to Northern California. His drinking worsened and he became a nonentity and the family's Invisible Man. When he was working, he would never come home on Friday night and disappear until time to go to work on Monday. He had become a weekend binge drinker.

In Aldredge's words, "I had some respect for him because he was my father. Just because he was my father. My mother said, 'I don't get along with him. He's not supporting us, but I don't want you to go around hating your father. We're not going to be doing that. I'll handle that part of it.' When he was there, especially during the week when he worked, he was OK. He really was a bright guy."

Aldredge's mother also gave her boys a plan for survival: "You can see your father isn't helping out, so you boys have to take care of your school clothes and all the incidentals at school, and I'll be doing housework and working with you in the fields."

Mrs. Aldredge washed and ironed her sons' clothes until they were in high school, although occasionally, John and Jim did do ironing. The boys had household chores like carrying out the garbage every day. They would rotate washing the dishes, making up their beds and sweeping the floors, also every day. Mrs. Aldredge said it loud and clear: "Nobody has servants in this house, so we'll have to work together on a daily basis."

Perhaps her orders were strict, but they were straight from the heart, and the boys sensed it. With all the work to be done, there was little time for hugs and kisses on the cheek, but the boys felt their mother's love, and they loved each other.

Her tough love taught Aldredge discipline, and he obeyed the rules and orders at school and on the playground. "If you acted out of line or got into trouble, my mother would whip you on your behind," he said. "As a little kid, she would tell you to stop crying while whipping you, which made you cry even more. You were always in a 'Catch-22.' You either got the misdemeanor or corporal punishment of a whipping. That was a problem."

He recalled how the corporal punishment would be meted out by his mother. She demanded that he would never commit such-and-such an offense again. But then she said, "I believe you will do it again."

"No, I never will."

"Then you are calling me a liar."

And here came 10 more swats.

The urge was to run. In fact, Aldredge said, "She would dare you to run. So I was in another 'Catch-22.'"

Once when he was too young to go to school, he heard a new word, and he thought he knew what it meant. He decided to try out the word. "All I saw was some spoiled fruit in a jar, but I called it 'piss in a jar.' Piss sounded like an OK description to me," he said, laughing. "However, the swats from my mother deleted that word from my vocabulary."

Another time, his mother was baby-sitting a little girl who lived next door to them in Richmond. The girl scribbled all over pages in Jim's coloring book. He announced in tears that he was going next door and tell the girl's mother what she had done to his book.

Mrs. Aldredge said, "You will not go and tell the little girl's mother anything." But Jim went anyway and got the whipping of his life.

Such discipline never diminished the love they had for each other.

Chapter Thirteen

"THIS JACKASS"

On the weekends, the three chopped cotton and picked grapes. Often brother John would work alone, and Jim would work with his mother, pulling the cotton sack for her because she suffered from varicose veins, so bad that amputation was later considered. Aldredge says: "Through the will of God and much prayer, amputation never occurred."

Whatever money the boys made working they kept. That was another one of her rules, but she did instruct them that they had to tithe to the church out of their money.

Mrs. Aldredge was determined not to go on welfare, though, at times, they weren't far from it. Their strong, loving bond helped them through, along with occasional help with vegetables from neighbors. She always made certain they had enough food, even if it was only fried Irish potatoes, biscuits and syrup. Jim never ate a steady diet of meat until his senior year in high school. She purchased most of her groceries at the Cherry Avenue Auction, about two miles from where they lived, and made butter by shaking cream in a jar.

As the father's drinking worsened, Aldredge said the three learned to tip-toe around him in an egg-shell truce. They never invited anyone to the house because they knew the father would come in and throw them out of his house. That meant there were never any relatives showing up for Thanksgiving or Christmas dinner, or even presents. In fact, holidays for them were working days. "On Thanksgiving day, we would get up early in the morning and work in the fields until about 5 p.m. And then, we would come home, and my mother would boil a chicken, make cornbread dressing and black-eyed peas. Of course, there was no cranberry sauce, which, sadly at that time, was considered a budget-buster. That was basically it. So to this day, I just look at every day as Thanksgiving—Thanksgiving in the sense of my daily gratitude to God for His grace. In fact, all holidays were bad times for us because of my father's penchant for acting a fool."

Aldredge believes that the bigger and better he and his brother became at sports, the worse his father became, threatening to throw pots or complaining about the food or anything else that irritated him and lit his fuse.

While the father's drunken outbursts were usually only vocal, there was one time when he shoved Aldredge and another time when his brother buried him in the ground as a lineman would pile-drive a quarterback. They were shooting baskets at their homemade hoop in their bare, hardpan yard. The old man stormed out of the house and said they were stirring up dust and making too much noise.

Aldredge reconstructed the play-by-play like a TV football announcer: "My brother said, 'We're not doing anything.' He said, 'I said you were.' He went over and shoved my brother. My brother, being a football player, grabbed him with both arms and dumped him on his head. He went plop! on the ground and his eyes rolled. I said, 'Oh, no, he's killed the guy.' He went uhhnnn. We didn't know what the heck to do—there was no 9-1-1. Finally he came out of it."

But fight his father? "Never."

The more independent Mrs. Aldredge and the two boys became, the worse the father became when having to "play catch-up."

Years later, he asked his mother why they didn't leave earlier. "My mother had this philosophy: 'Because I didn't want you boys to have a stepfather. It was my belief when once you got married, you stayed there. None of this divorce stuff, and I didn't want to embarrass you kids.' That was her reason, so she tolerated everything."

The father saw Aldredge play football twice, but only because Mrs. Aldredge was going to one game in Hanford and to a Fresno City schools' football carnival, and never on his own. And for sure he never saw Aldredge play baseball.

He did know his sons played sports and were doing well because the neighbors would tell him of their accomplishments, but he never asked them how they were doing. Aldredge and John hid their teams' schedules from him, afraid he'd show up at a game drunk.

Once when he was drunk and on a tear, he threatened to kick his own sons out of his house. Only 14 at the time, Aldredge told him, "If you let us stay here, then as soon as I graduate from high school, I'll pay you all of the rent back." The father let them stay.

Or the brothers might set him off by asking him for something. Aldredge says, "He wanted us to ask for something so he could turn us down abruptly and with cuss words."

When Aldredge was in the ninth grade and playing football, his father made a frightening threat: "I'll go right up to that high school and have you taken off those teams." Aldredge's seat in the classroom was usually next to the windows, and he kept nervously looking out to see whether his father was goose-stepping double-time up the street. "This fool might just do it at any time. He never came up, but he threatened to take us off the team. I'm young, and what do I know?" Even so, Aldredge knew he had to get his mother out of the house and out of the marriage.

*   *   *

Forget the time-worn adage about how the apple falls close to the tree. The young Aldredge vowed never to repeat his father's alcoholism and resisted the temptation, even in professional baseball. It's an all-too-sad story that players leave the clubhouse after a night game and make a bee line to the hotel bar—some for booze, some for women. True, Aldredge might go to the bar with teammates, but he would order a 7 UP with a cherry to give the impression that he was drinking vodka. It effectively curtailed his being needled because he supposedly wasn't man enough to drink. The fact is, he was underage.

*   *   *

His father most likely never knew about Alcoholics Anonymous and wouldn't have tried to sober up anyway. Like many alcoholics, he never thought he had a problem. Like most alcoholics, they drink their way to the grave. Aldredge said: "I didn't know of any professional help." And: "A person must be willing to change in order to solve most problems. My father did not choose to change. He got worse."

The father played the martyr role to the hilt, saying, "When I die, you can just stick me over in the corner and put two-by-fours over my head. I don't give a damn."

He died of a heart attack at age 47 in April 1959, the same year of Aldredge's first comeback attempt in baseball. Before he died, he had made some sort of peace with John Aldredge. John had married and bought a house. The old man was living in a room out back. John, who owned a couple of trucks, hired him to help haul cantaloupes on the west side of the San Joaquin Valley. Saying the funeral was too sad for him and he couldn't handle it, John did not attend.

Aldredge went with his mother to the funeral home. Friends and family viewing the body were crying and wailing how he is such a nice guy. Aldredge said flatly: "No, he's not." To Aldredge, his father was not a nice guy, alive or dead. Neither Aldredge nor his mother approached the casket.

The funeral service was held on a weekday morning, and, when it came time to go to the cemetery, Mrs. Aldredge stepped in and told Aldredge: "You're not going to miss your afternoon class. I'll go out to the cemetery because we have friends and relatives from Stockton, and all this heavy grief stuff is just for this jackass, as far as I'm concerned."

After the trip to the cemetery, his mother entertained their kinfolks at home, then bade them goodbye and sent them off. Aldredge was 19 years old but Mrs. Aldredge was still in charge. He didn't miss class at Fresno City College.

* * *

"Your education comes first because I couldn't finish mine, and I'm telling you, you've got to get an education. You can't be fooling around." Mrs. Aldredge's words still ring in Aldredge's ears.

As soon as he was graduated from high school in 1956, Aldredge enrolled at Fresno City College for summer classes and played for the school's fall baseball team.

In spring 1957, at spring training in Anaheim, the Pirates' Branch Rickey Jr. invited him to play in the Winter Leagues in Mexico and the Caribbean after the season, but Aldredge told him politely: "No, I don't want to go down there. When the season is over in San Jose, I'm going home. I'll be registering a little late, but I'm going to go to City College. I want to get an education. It's something I promised my mother anyway."

Chapter Fourteen

RECRUITED TO TEACH BIBLE LESSONS

The family had moved from the migrant camp in Calwa to a second camp on 10 acres at the corner of Church and Cherry avenues in 1947, and Aldredge was enrolled at Kirk Elementary School. He showed an early penchant for learning as he absorbed his older brother's homework lessons. John was 2½ years older. Aldredge knew the alphabet, could count to 100 and could read well. Besides, playing in the sand box bored him. He enjoyed his first academic success, and the school moved him up from the third grade to the fourth grade. He was put in the elite "Blue Bird" reading group. Aldredge attributes his progress to his being a good listener. Around that time—age 8 or 9—he consciously made a decision to be somebody by planning and setting goals, no matter how hard he had to work. He always has been fond of quoting the essence of his philosophy: "Positive hustle marks toward a goal are keys to one's success, in spite of opposition and hardship. You've got to have a plan and a set of goals to guide your actions and efforts."

*   *   *

Their mother also was keeping tabs on her sons' social and spiritual development. They had to meet her daily hygiene test or, in her words, the "smell test." Before they left for school in the morning, she made sure they had brushed their teeth and had washed under their arms. Aldredge said: "She always said that she did not want us smelling like goats out in public." When they failed her test, the remedy was baking soda, maybe the whole box.

During this time, not only was he heeding his mother's first admonition about getting an education, but he also was paying close attention to her second: "Stay close to God by counting on prayer and faith in good times and bad." Having no access to a car, she insisted that they walk four miles to the North Avenue Church of God in Christ and back home every Sunday—and sometimes twice on Sunday, if they didn't stay over at the church. She taught adult Sunday school classes, and Aldredge was recruited to teach classes to children from kindergarten through third grade, barely younger than him, because the adults refused to take the assignment. That's when he started to comprehend the principles of teaching, never realizing he would devote 40 years of his life to educational instruction.

"I was about 10 years old with no real understanding of the Bible," he recalled. "But I was able and comfortable with reading the little story on the back of a Bible card with such biblical characters as Samson, David and Jesus, and interpreting the picture on the other side of the card, such as this big, strong man, Samson, pulling down the pillars of the temple or David slaying Goliath or Noah and the ark.

Add up their experiences already—poverty, racism and an alcoholic father, the Aldredge brothers had undeniable evidence that they would need God and his grace to come out the other side wholly intact. For their part, they were learning a tenacious work ethic. All of this was captured in another admonition from their mother: try, try, try and work, work, work, and then leave the rest to God.

Chapter Fifteen

Mr. Crandle

If Mrs. Aldredge made certain her sons were squeaky clean before they left for school, Jim Aldredge was checked again when he and his classmates faced Mr. James Crandle at the start of the day at Kirk Elementary School.

Mr. Crandle was the first *real* teacher who blossomed Jim Aldredge.

Mr. Crandle conducted morning inspection for clean fingernails and brushed teeth. In the classroom, he emphasized reading, writing and arithmetic, and then there were daily discussions about current issues that would pique the minds of fifth- and sixth-grade students. During morning recess, Mr. Crandle had the boys do calisthenics. He picked Aldredge and his friend, Joe Williams, to lead the exercises. The girls had their own group and individual exercises.

Certainly Mr. Crandle was strict, but only because he cared about his pupils. Such a role model was what young Jim Aldredge needed and wanted. "I welcomed a positive adult role model badly at the time. Mr. Crandle more than filled the bill"—at precisely the right time.

Aldredge knew of a youngster who tried to join the Cub Scout troop across the street from the school and was rejected. No blacks. Mr. Crandle recognized the injustice and took matters into his own hands by going to the YMCA and forming a Gray Y club at Kirk so the black and Mexican-American kids could go to camp for one week in the Sierra Nevada at Lake Tulare/Sequoia.

Another special extracurricular activity he began was Christmas caroling through the neighborhoods of Germantown.

Mr. Crandle organized basketball, soccer and softball teams at Kirk, and spearheaded competition with such other nearby elementary schools as Jane Addams, Lincoln and Columbia. Aldredge competed in each of those sports. Then, Mr. Crandle urged him to run track in the annual YMCA Pow-Wow at Roeding Park against clubs throughout the Valley. Admittedly a chubby kid, Aldredge wasn't a fast runner, but he didn't mind because his buddies were also-rans to the fastest runner in their class—a girl. She also was the first batter when she beat them to home plate for a game of workups during the lunch recess. Once he got there second, and two bullies pushed him out of line.

The bullying continued into summer vacation against Aldredge, as quiet as a dormant volcano. One of the bullies tried to take Aldredge's patched-together bicycle. He grabbed the handle bars and was caught defenseless when Aldredge jumped off the bike, swinging his fists wildly and with power in the bully's face. He proved that a bully will cave in when challenged. The bully quickly backed off, laughing nervously and saying he was only kidding.

Aldredge would remember one of the bullies years later.

Nevertheless, his desire to play baseball had begun. When he saw a photograph of Jackie Robinson in the Pittsburgh Courier[9] newspaper with a headline saying "Double Play," his interest grew. The money he earned working in the fields let him spend $1 each year for a baseball cap. Mr. Crandle saw his potential and, for encouragement, lent him a book, "The Southpaw From San Francisco." Aldredge read it in three days and returned it.

Mr. Crandle also was a calming influence when Aldredge had the jitters before a game or a test. Encouraging and supportive words made everything easier. Once Aldredge had the flu, and Mr. Crandle came to visit him two days in a row. "He came to see how I was doing. That really impressed my mother. And he certainly was not the school nurse."

Before Aldredge was graduated from the sixth grade at Kirk, the family lived in a city migrant camp, but then moved into the "real house" on the 3⅓ acres of cotton land. Aldredge did not want to stop going to a good school or his teacher, Mr. Crandle. His solution was to ride his wobbly bicycle from his house in the Fresno Colony School District to Kirk Elementary. School officials never knew.

---

[9] The original Pittsburgh Courier (1907-1965) was one of the largest and most influential newspapers catering to African-Americans. It became a weekly and was renamed the New Pittsburgh Courier in 1966.

Chapter Sixteen

EVERYBODY CAN PLAY

Aldredge's desire to play baseball started with those simple softball games in elementary school, and he was soon ahead of his playmates. The family's move from the Calwa migrant camp into the Fresno Unified School District and near the Cosmos Playground meant the opportunities to play were greater, the competition stiffer and the chance to improve better.

John Toomasian, the former basketball coach at Edison High School and Fresno City College, remembers those days at Cosmos. "I coached a team of eighth-grade baseball players and, although Jim was only in the sixth grade, he batted fourth on the team. He could really hit the ball. Jim also was a fierce competitor. If he had a dislike, he hated to lose. And I liked kids like that." The other coach was Lowell Reynolds.

During 1949 and 1950, Aldredge played for the Cosmos team in a competitive playground league called "Peanut Baseball League." Opponents were from Frank H. Ball, California Field and Fink-White playgrounds. The league was sponsored by the Fresno Recreation Department. The winning players were treated to a 10-cent ice cream cone—that was two scoops, and whoever hit a home run, win or lose, was rewarded with a 25-cent milkshake.

* * *

Not much later, the Aldredge brothers began going with their mother, as second-generation migrant camp dwellers, to pick grapes and cotton in "about every vineyard and cotton field in Fresno County." Aldredge called it "backbreaking and dirty." He already was determined to make some money and eventually remove his mother from a bad marriage. He was in the eighth grade and only 12, but he was methodical about the effort it would take: plowing the cotton field with a mule, practicing football with John in the plowed field, swinging a loaded bat that was twice as heavy as his normal bat and relying on his faith in God.

*   *   *

When official Little League baseball came to Fresno, service clubs like the Lions, Elks, Rotary and Kiwanis began sponsoring teams in west Fresno. Aldredge tried out for pitcher and overpowered batters. At the plate he pounded the ball. Unfortunately, Aldredge was ruled ineligible because he didn't live inside the city limit. Coaches who were hoping he could pitch for them were sorely disappointed. One coach even challenged the ruling during the tryouts and selected Aldredge anyway in case the issue of residency was reversed in his favor. The West Fresno Little League president advised Aldredge to keep practicing in case something worked out, and he was allowed to practice with the team that selected him first as a pitcher until the first game of the season. But it became evident that the president knew all along that Aldredge would not play.

*   *   *

Despite the disappointment, Aldredge turned it into a positive, and he has never forgotten the importance of the four civic clubs in establishing the West Fresno Little League. He put the memory into practice later as a playground leader who could change the life of an underprivileged kid through sports.

In the 1960s after his baseball career ended, when Aldredge worked for the Fresno Parks and Recreation Department, he created a Playground Baseball League specifically for the kids who had not been selected by the West Fresno Little League or by Babe Ruth League teams.

His longtime friend, the Rev. Harry Miller, said, "It was a league that gave hope and joy to kids who felt deprived of both because they were not selected to play on any of the eight teams in Little League and Babe Ruth leagues in west Fresno."

He spoke of the irony of Little League and Babe Ruth leagues that are designed to give youths a place to go, to learn teamwork, to develop camaraderie, to make good moral choices and to simply have fun. "Yet, when you cut a kid from Little League or Babe Ruth, you are telling them point-blank that he or she is not good enough, and you create the opposite effect as you toss these kids back out into the unorganized and sometimes illegal elements of our society."

Aldredge would not accept a young child *not* being able to play. He decided to redirect the path that many spurned youngsters often followed as they left his playground, downcast, and eventually for the criminal activities of gambling, prostitution and drugs in nearby Chinatown. That's when he created the Playground Baseball League at Fink-White Playground. Players were branded as the rag-tags and have-nots.

The league featured five teams of rejected players who had to use old gloves and bats and balls—and share them with the other team after one side was out. Aldredge acquired the equipment when teams across town replaced theirs. His league still was without full uniforms, but discarded jerseys of every color and stripe did fine.

* * *

On one particular day, Aldredge made the biggest player in his rag-tag league, Larry Willis, the catcher for all the teams.

After a while, Willis pleaded, "Coach, can I please have an at-bat?"

Every few innings, Willis got to bat and then went back behind the plate.

There was another player who could catch, but often he had to pitch for two teams—because at least he could throw the ball over the plate.

As the league's coach and umpire, Aldredge noticed Willis had bruises all over his body, taking the beating catchers take from foul tips, blocking pitches and collisions. By then, Willis said he enjoyed catching because that's where the action is. He improved and became a good ballplayer. Willis also continued in sports and became a coach with the Edison High varsity football team.

Aldredge issued these league rules: Everybody would play, and there would be no criticism, arguing or fussing if somebody struck out or misplayed a ball in the field. He told them that even big league players make errors. "So enjoy yourselves, but always try hard," he told them.

The players developed pride in themselves—and in their mismatched jerseys, wearing them every day, game or no game.

Today, the civic club sponsorships have gone. However, the Edison Babe Ruth League has continued and expanded under different sponsorships, including Aldredge's. Since 2005, he has sponsored two teams and Reviving Baseball to the Inner City (RBI) through the Dr. James E. Aldredge Foundation.

Chapter Seventeen

THE LURE OF SPORTS

Coming clearly through the Sunday night air were the whine and the roar of another sport. He and his brother could hear the sounds from the auto racing track, not far from their house. Auto racing had caught Aldredge's fancy. He was still determined to be somebody, and driving a race car might be the ticket. He and John were so set on attending the races that they got jobs sweeping the grandstands for free admission. For a little work, compared with what they were used to doing, they saw Billy Vukovich[10] and brother Eli, and their friend, Edgar Elder, race midgets.

Aldredge said, "Unfortunately, or maybe fortunately, the closest I ever came to being a race car driver was racing bicycles around our house with my brother, John, and neighborhood kids. Our bicycles were modified with seven sprocket bike chains, which were the fastest on the market. Keep in mind that the 'track' around our house was easy to make because the house didn't have sidewalks, curbs, driveways or lawns. The house was surrounded by dirt. There were no yard improvements and no flowers." And racing in the family's beat-up 1936 V-8 Ford was out of the question.

A more likely sport—professional football—gave them additional inspiration, and on fall Sunday afternoons after church, the brothers would walk two miles to Joe Williams' house and watch the San Francisco 49ers with Y.A. Tittle, Joe Perry, Hugh McElhenny, John Henry Johnson and Billy Wilson.

---

[10]   Vukovich won the Indianapolis 500 in 1953 and 1954, and was leading in 1955 when he was killed on the 57th lap.

Aldredge's favorite 49er was defensive end Charlie Powell who went directly from high school to the Stockton Ports baseball team in 1952 and then to the National Football League that fall. Aldredge thought: "If I tried hard, prayed and worked hard, I might be able to do the same in baseball." Five years later, Aldredge did.

*   *   *

After the sixth grade at Kirk Elementary, Aldredge's sports path was interrupted for two years. He enrolled in Edison Junior High School, and his quest to be somebody was so strong that he took beginning band and selected the trumpet. He had seen a magazine picture of Louis Armstrong playing the horn. He was at the junior high for three weeks when Fresno Unified School District officials discovered Aldredge's county address was Route 6, Box 676 at 2457 South Walnut Avenue beyond the boundaries of the Fresno school district. He was sent to Fresno Colony Middle School in the county. His dream of being the next "Satchmo" didn't return with him, and he suddenly was three weeks behind in classroom work and without organized athletics. The school had none. The basketball hoops were two feet short of regulation and potential sport fields only weeds.

Aldredge said: "Although my faith in God and the fact that the grace of God had no bounds, it was difficult to witness so much student-athletic potential and time being wasted at the county school." He blamed the school administration's apathy.

Aldredge found a productive outlet by competing at the YMCA's High-Y Club. The adult volunteer adviser was the Rev. Chester Riggins of the Saints Rest Baptist Church near Kirk Elementary.

Aldredge was correct about the potential greatness in the Fresno Colony. Years later, such Olympic athletes as Randy Williams and Maxie Parks came out of the area. Williams won a gold medal in the long jump in the 1972 Munich Olympics, and Parks won a gold medal in the 4-by-400-meter relay in the 1976 Montreal Olympics. Former National Basketball Association players Roscoe and Clifford Pondexter also came from Fresno Colony.

As Aldredge continued to try to be somebody, he did achieve that goal in one respect, according to Roscoe Pondexter. "Jim Aldredge was one of the first role models I had way before I even got a chance to meet him. My mother told me about his career and the person that Jim Aldredge was, and it was nothing but respect. She and others told me about baseball and how good he was in school way before I knew who he was. He is still a trailblazer, and I have nothing but respect for the brother. He has done a lot of good."

Chapter Eighteen

EDISON HIGH AT LAST

More obstacles were going to demand more perseverance and patience from Aldredge, and they were right around the bend for the eager athlete when he entered Edison High School in fall 1952. At age 13, Aldredge thought he could simply go out for football, basketball and baseball. In football, his best opportunity would be as a lineman. The backfield positions were filled with speedsters from the school's championship-caliber track and field team.

Not only was he big for his age, but he also had been tested in the field—literally—playing tackle football—minus pads and helmets—in neighbor games in the plowed field behind his house. Brother John, a lineman, and running back J.C. White saw he had the moxie and talent to compete against varsity players and prodded him to show up for the team's preseason practices.

Encouragement from them boosted Aldredge's confidence, and it soared higher as he held his own against older and experienced linemen in practice. His hopes of playing for the varsity were turning into reality. He quickly rose to second-string guard and second-string linebacker.

After two weeks of practice, there was no question about his ability, but the coach had others in mind. How old are you? What grade are you in? What is your address? He forthrightly told them he was 13. That was too young to play varsity.

Aldredge had an answer for that. He simply volunteered to play on the B team.

A check of school records answered the others. Because he lived outside the Fresno city limit, he wasn't allowed to attend Edison Junior High as a seventh-grader. He simply hoped the residency issue would go away by the time he reached the senior high school.

The principal called him into his office and said: "Jim, you live on Route 6, Box 676, on Walnut Avenue, which is outside of the Fresno Unified School District. That means you will have to attend Washington Union High School." It was the designed progression for a graduate of Fresno Colony Elementary and Middle Schools.

For some reason, Aldredge was not intimidated. He firmly told the principal: "If I can't play for Edison, I want my insurance and towel fee money back that I paid this summer." It was hard-earned money he made that summer from chopping cotton.

Momentarily deflecting the demand, the Edison principal curiously asked Aldredge: "How are you doing in football?"

"Pretty good," Aldredge quietly answered, explaining he was second string on defense and offense.

The principal listened politely but phoned the football coaches. They verified Aldredge's honest answer. The principal told him he could stay at Edison and be reunited with his brother, John, who was starting his fourth year in the school district. Older brother had set the residency precedent for the Aldredge family.

"Then," Aldredge wanted to know, "can I go back to practice and play right away?"

"Yes," the principal said. "And good luck."

*   *   *

Nevertheless, playing with the varsity would have to wait until he was 15. That was the age requirement. At least Aldredge was at Edison, and that was what mattered.

Oddly, his preseason success didn't make any difference to the B team coach who thought Aldredge was arrogant. Wasn't it Aldredge who suggested being dropped to the B team? Aldredge rode the bench that season and played only two minutes. Again, logic and justice were elusive.

Aldredge didn't get his dauber down, kept his grades up, was never late to practice and never missed a practice. He thought: "This too shall pass. You've got to keep going in spite of everything, if you want to be somebody and succeed. Through prayer, faith in God and yourself, you can make a rough road smooth."

When football finished, the next hurdle was B team basketball. Guess who was coaching the team? The B team football coach. Aldredge was cut after a few tryout practices. For an unexplainable reason, the coach asked him back two weeks later. Aldredge then rode the bench again—but justifiably, he said. "Unlike in football, my basketball skills had diminished when I attended the Fresno Colony Middle School in the seventh and eighth grades, and I could not make up the ground at Edison, which was rich in basketball stars and a winning tradition." The team went on to win the Valley championship, giving Aldredge a winning attitude, though he had only five minutes of playing time.

*   *   *

In fall 1953, his sophomore year, Aldredge started three preseason football games at offensive guard. At linebacker, he called defensive signals but admits there was one problem: Sanger High quarterback Tom Flores[11] picked apart the defense with his passing. Sanger won by two touchdowns.

That was preseason, and, when league play began, Aldredge the sophomore was demoted to the practice team because he was still one year too young to play varsity football. The California Interscholastic Federation rules hadn't changed, and 15 was still the minimum age. On the scout team, he played running back and played on the defensive line.

That was one lesson, and another one was yet to come. Fortunately, it was dealt by his brother, John. It was tough love, with a dollop of brotherly love. "One of the first days that we practiced together at Edison during the preseason, John hurt and helped me all on the same play. He walloped me. Then after he knocked my block off and before I could say a word after the play, John said in his bass voice, 'Remember, man, you don't have no friends on the gridiron.'"

John had given him a similar lesson when they were in elementary school and Aldredge thought he had what it takes to become a world

---

[11] Flores went on to Fresno City College and the then-College of the Pacific on an academic scholarship. He played for the Oakland Raiders, and coached the Raiders to two Super Bowl victories, the first over the Philadelphia Eagles, the second over the Washington Redskins.

boxing champion like Joe Louis or Henry Armstrong. He challenged John to a round of sparring. John popped him in the head so quickly and so hard that "my thoughts of a boxing career almost instantly vanished but, unfortunately, the pain lasted a couple of hours."

*   *   *

Aldredge is proud of his brother who played at Fresno City College with Flores, who was named most valuable player in his sophomore season. When Flores moved on to COP[12], John was chosen the team's MVP, a rare honor for a lineman. He is considered one of the best linemen in school history. In 1997, John was selected to the Wall of Fame at Fresno City College. Jim accepted the posthumous award for John at the Wall of Fame banquet, which was attended by Mrs. Aldredge; John's widow, Ora; and their three children, Freda, Gaylon and Carrie.

That was the first year for the athletic Wall of Fame, and Aldredge was on the selection committee. The other six committee members nominated him, too, but Aldredge firmly turned down the idea, saying, "It would have been a great honor, but I was not going to create a possibility for someone to question my selection based on my being on the committee and have that spill over and take away anything from the other Wall of Honor inductees."

It was only a matter of time before Aldredge would receive a similar honor—not for sports, but for academics. On February 26, 2009, he took his place on the Academic and Community Service Wall of Fame at the African-American Museum. At the induction ceremony, Master of Ceremonies Dorothy "Dottie" Smith, a longtime trustee on the State Center Community College board, praised Aldredge for his contributions to the African-American community.

*   *   *

Baseball was relief from a trying fall when spring semester 1953 rolled around, and Aldredge tried out for varsity and made the team—only one of four freshmen chosen. He had not yet turned 14.

---

[12] College of the Pacific became the University of the Pacific in 1961.

At the start, he saw limited duty with two players ahead of him in left field. The first-stringer wasn't hitting, and then he misplayed a ground ball to left. He was replaced by another upperclassman who botched two easy pop flies. Aldredge took his place, hit above .300 for the season and never made an error. He jokes now, though observers would say it's no joke: "I could hit 'em and go get 'em, slide on both sides, field with the rain and sleet in my face, and stroke an easy .300."

MISS PATRICIA DUNKLEE

With the beginning of athletic success at Edison, it wasn't long before word started getting around about Aldredge's talents. He first attracted the interest of Miss Patricia Dunklee, his teacher in first period. Baseball scouts would catch on soon. But her interest was two-fold: first academics, then athletics. She became his dedicated classroom adviser and wasted little time telling him his freshman year was a bust academically.

She is the second teacher who entered Aldredge's life at the perfect time and helped to blossom him.

Aldredge's brother, John, had pushed him toward an education in the industrial arts. John's philosophy was to take classes that he could "get by on" and maintain his football eligibility as a standout player. He was called "Big Hoss," and for good reason. John was selected to the All-League and All-City teams in his junior and senior years—leading up to his impressive years at City College.

Little brother complied with big brother's advice: "Don't take those difficult classes because those high school students are real smart." So Aldredge took the easy way out and enrolled in shop classes and in other classes that aren't college prep.

Miss Dunklee appeared in his sophomore year and immediately reversed Aldredge's future. She knew his grades were good in all his core classes, and she knew he was a good athlete. She was a sports fan and had a friend who played at Cal Poly San Luis Obispo.

"She told me: 'You're really good. I was watching you play the other day. If you keep that up, you could get a scholarship.' Scholarship? What's that? My mother didn't know, and I doubt that my father knew.

"She said: 'If you get real good grades and keep playing baseball the way you are, you could play at Cal Poly, and I've seen you play football, too. You could go to Cal Poly for free.' I said, 'No kidding?!'

"She said: 'So here's what we have to do. We have to get you into college-prep courses. Now let's figure something out. Next semester, rather than Metal Shop 2, go back and take Algebra 1.'

"I went back and took classes with underclassmen in my junior and senior years because I had left out a whole bunch of subjects. I continued to be in her advisory class because she asked for me. We'd work out my schedules, and she'd come out to see our games and say, 'You're doing good!' Then she heard about the pro scouts coming around and said, 'I told you so!'

"And I had said, 'But there are smart Oriental students in there.' She said, 'It doesn't make any difference. Go in there, work hard and you'll be all right.' I hung in there with them, but my brother and J.C. White had me scared. They didn't even know what H_2O was!"

Miss Dunklee watched Aldredge's grades improve and never wavered from her commitment to him, stressing grades first, athletics second. With her encouragement in that sophomore season, he anchored the baseball team in centerfield and batted over .300. And he had a new goal: to win the Fresno B'nai B'rith Student-Athlete award. "That's when I became a student-athlete," he said.

In his senior season of football, Aldredge won the team's Academic Award. He was named First Team All-Central California, First Team All-North Yosemite League and First Team All-City. In baseball, he missed the team's Academic Award by one vote—when he did not vote for himself to break a tie vote by his teammates.

*　　*　　*

Edison did not have an American Legion team the next summer, so Aldredge played for the Washington Union team. It turned out to be perfect because the schedule allowed him to continue working in the fields. Practices were held at 6:30 p.m. during the week, and games were on Saturday night and Sunday afternoon. Other Washington Union players also had to work pitching watermelons, working in fruit packing sheds, chopping cotton or hauling hay.

*   *   *

Having seemingly bided his time in the football trenches his first two years, Aldredge was gaining useful experience, and he quickly stood out when he finally could play as a 15-year-old junior. He was without equal as an offensive guard, opening holes for fleet running back Vestee Jackson.

While some stories about Aldredge's prowess in this book are impressive, it is his turn to tell about one of Jackson's legendary runs for the Fresno City College Rams:

"One particular play against Reedley College in the Conference Junior College Championship game is talked about to this day. Fortunately, the game was filmed providing proof that the mythical play is no myth. Vestee really made the unimaginable happen. Vestee, contrary to many running backs, relished delivering blows to defensive players the Jim Brown way. He broke 12 tackles en route to an 80-yard touchdown run for City College. Now, I figure you might be wondering, 'How could Vestee break 12 tackles when there are only 11 defensive players allowed on the field at a time?' Well, Vestee was actually searching for opposing defensive players to run over during the entire play, and he broke away from one of the opposing players twice. That defensive player was also pulled into the end zone when Jackson grabbed his shoulder pad and then politely let him go at the goal line."

*   *   *

As an Edison linebacker, Aldredge called defensive signals because coaches in his first two years recognized his mental acuity. Not only was he versatile, but he also was durable, and he played every down in his junior season. In football, he was named All-City, All-League for the North Yosemite League and All-Central Valley. As a senior, Aldredge repeated those three honors. Again, he didn't miss a down all season. In baseball, he duplicated those awards and was named Edison's most valuable player twice.

COACH MARTY SANTIGIAN

If Miss Dunklee was encouraging Aldredge about education *from the classroom*, his line coach was encouraging him about education *from the football field*.

Coach Marty Santigian is the fourth teacher who blossomed Aldredge in his rise out of poverty.

Santigian could not speak English when his family arrived in America. By the fourth grade, he had picked up enough English to reach grade-level status. Meanwhile, his family was living barely above the poverty line.

Aldredge knew what that was like, and he knew he was in constant fear that his father would yank him off the Edison football team. Santigian became his coach and his surrogate father who helped him to cope, develop a positive self-image and succeed.

Aldredge also knew that Santigian was for real. Santigian had earned a scholarship to Pepperdine College and became an All-American middle guard in football. As an immigrant, Santigian also had faced racism, so he understood that, too. Santigian said: "Jim, the only way you can overcome all this stuff is with an education because they can't take it away from you."

Santigian later earned a Ph.D. and thus became a crucial influence on Aldredge long after high school. "Even after I came back from baseball, he would say, 'See, Jim, education was important. I told you to continue it.' I'd gone on to get a doctorate, and I'd see him and tell him he was right."

*   *   *

Every day at football practice, there were always those punishing contact drills, the 2-on-1 drill. Aldredge had heard about one player, just up from the B team, and how that player had been bullying and injuring several freshmen and sophomore players with cheap shots. He had seen the rookie around the locker room, but didn't let on that he recognized him. Then, he conveniently arranged to team, side by side, with Walter "The Bear" Jones in practice. The bully hadn't learned anything and was just as obtuse as he was six years earlier—when he had pushed Aldredge out of line during the softball games and then tried to take his bicycle.

Aldredge was on a mission to whip the bully decisively, and they gave him an unforgettable licking. Aldredge described it as "social justice."

*   *   *

In Aldredge's senior baseball year, scouts began knocking on his door. Ten of the 16 major league teams were interested in the 16-year-old. They could read the stats: no errors. They had seen Edison's all-dirt, hard-pan field. Without grass, there were no soft bounces. Let a ball hit the ground and it would jack-rabbit past outfielders for a home run. While opposing outfielders played deep to cut off balls hit into the gap, they couldn't play deep enough. His home runs simply went over their heads.

His power opened scouts' eyes, and they knew of his All-League honors in both sports, and they had seen him play on the KMJ Radio and Television and The Fresno Bee All-Star Baseball School team for three summers. He was able to squeeze in the baseball school between chopping cotton. No one had a ride for him to the school, conducted at Fresno State College Park, so he rode the city bus to the school, paying for tokens purchased with his field wages.

His first attempt was a flop at age 14, in 1953. To the top players trying out (including future Atlanta Brave manager Bobby Cox from Selma), he must have looked like "Shoeless Joe from Hannibal, Mo." Wearing a T-shirt and jeans, he wasn't dressed for success. He had an old pair of spikes he bought the year before, and his glove was a second-hand Rawlings model given to him two years earlier by his American Legion coach in Easton. The margin of error was exactly one, and, when a bad hop kicked off his glove, he recovered too late with a weak throw to first base, and it was over. Never mind that he was out of his regular position at second base. He would have to wait until the next year.

He vowed to return in 1954 when he still would be among the youngest players trying out. This time, he made the most of a second opportunity, playing flawlessly in centerfield and wearing pants and stirrup stockings he borrowed from the American Legion team. At bat, he hit with power and did not strike out.

Quickly gaining a reputation as a good hitter, he never saw a good pitch to hit. Pitchers tried to pitch around him, but he refused to walk, instantly becoming an excellent bad-ball hitter. He was the Fresno version of the typical Caribbean player who must produce at the plate if he ever wants a chance to get off the island. "I could have walked, and I'm not sure I ever got a good pitch. I was swinging at balls two feet outside. If I always walked, I'd never hit a ball, and they'd never give me a team jacket."

Making the team meant receiving a classy letterman's jacket with leather sleeves, like the one he couldn't afford to buy at school. He treasured one of those jackets. So, he hit his way into the Senior All-Star team's starting lineup and batted cleanup. He got the jacket, proudly wore it and expanded his minimal wardrobe by 34 percent. The first two, one gray and one maroon, were made by his mother.

By coming back after failing on his first try, being the youngest and having to scrape together money for the bus fare demonstrated his faith and perseverance. These experiences helped him to develop a leadership style of granting, rather than denying, opportunity and giving second chances. They also built on of his themes to live by: "Bad hops in life do happen to the best of us."

*   *   *

In the mid-1950s, Fresno High School produced a crop of notable ballplayers; namely, left-hander Dick Ellsworth, right-hander Jim Maloney and catcher Pat Corrales. The Society for Baseball Research considers the team one of the greatest California prep baseball teams of all time. Ellsworth won 22 games for the Chicago Cubs in 1963, and in the same year Maloney won 23 for the Cincinnati Reds. Maloney also threw two no-hitters in his career. Corrales had a nine-year career in the big leagues and was a long-time coach for the Atlanta Braves.

Understandably, the Edison High players at first were in awe of the Fresno High squad. After adjusting to the "big boys," they found they could compete. Fresno High might have been in a league of its own, but Edison High wasn't far behind.

The Fresno High group wasn't as oblivious to the talents of its opponents as Edison may have thought, especially Aldredge. Playing American Legion baseball in the summer, the Fresno High team actively sought the bat and arm of Aldredge. He had to turn them down because he had to work. If his father had helped the family financially, he wouldn't have had to chop cotton for 75 cents an hour. It would have allowed Aldredge to play Legion ball across town, and go to Stanford and play for Dutch Fehring's Indian teams. He never would have chosen professional baseball over a full scholarship to Stanford as a student-athlete, but he had to take care of his mother.

Chapter Nineteen

B'NAI B'RITH HEROES AND OTHERS

In his senior year at Edison, Aldredge won the football team's Academic Award, confirming the faith Miss Dunklee and coach Santigian had in him. He fell one vote shy of winning the same award for baseball. At the end of the school year, their dream—and his—came true when he won the B'nai B'rith award as the top student-athlete in Fresno for 1956. He came out above all the nominees from Roosevelt, Fresno and San Joaquin Memorial high schools.

The Edison High Athletic Department nominated him for the award and passed on its recommendation to the school principal. His classroom work was checked and confirmed, along with his extracurricular accomplishments as junior class vice president and student body president in his senior year. His athletic achievements also were there for everyone to see, and they helped with winning the award as much as anything else.

* * *

Winning the B'nai B'rith award is the one that made him the proudest. It also fulfilled his mother's admonition to try, try, try and try again, and keep the faith through prayer.

His father never knew about the award, never knew that his son was a candidate and certainly never knew about the award ceremony, a father-son banquet. Nobody in the family told him and weren't about to, afraid that he would show up drunk and disheveled, his preferred acts of antisocial behavior.

On the night of the banquet, Aldredge said, "I just left and went. One of the officials, Hy Ginsburg, asked if my dad was coming. I said he'd be here late because he's working on a car and can't get here. A little lie. Then, they said, 'Well, can you bring your brother?' I went and faked a phone call and told them I can't contact my brother either. So I was up there on the dais next to Bill Russell, K.C. Jones and miler John Landy. Russell and Jones had led the University of San Francisco to the second of two straight NCAA basketball championships and were competing in the West Coast Relays in the high jump. Landy, the Australian who was the second man to run a four-minute mile, presented Aldredge with the B'nai B'rith award.

As the chicken dinner was served, Aldredge began to dig in, but he was nervously trying to eat the chicken with a knife and fork. Russell saw him struggling. He gave Aldredge some fatherly advice: "Your hands were made before that knife and fork. So if you want to, you can eat that chicken if you use both hands at the same time. See, like this." Russell demonstrated the finger-lickin'-good technique and ate his chicken with both hands.

The entire evening was a fulfilling thrill for Aldredge: "It was big time." He held the leadership of the Fresno lodge, Ginsburg and Judge Leonard Meyers, in such high esteem that he became a part of the local leadership and served on the B'nai B'rith committee for 48 years, stepping down in 2008. He said it was time for someone else to have the opportunity to serve youths in the Fresno community.

*   *   *

As Edison High athletes gained respect and it became apparent they could compete against "the big boys," Aldredge's talents were making an impact on younger athletes coming up behind him in Fresno. His winning the B'nai B'rith award confirmed their reason to admire him, and the example he set after his baseball injury added to his credibility.

The term "role model" is in vogue these days but, then, the word was simply "hero," as if anyone would admit to having a hero or being a hero. Aldredge was a hero first to Harry Miller, four years his junior, who followed in his footsteps and made his mark first as an Edison athlete and then as the B'nai B'rith award winner in 1959.

Miller, who is the pastor of the Fresno Temple of God in Christ, credits Aldredge with inspiring him to become one of Fresno's most decorated high school athletes. Miller said Aldredge always was more than happy to pass on or point out what he learned to anyone he could by personal contact or his own example "He was ahead of his time," Miller remarked.

Other notable Edison baseball players who looked up to Aldredge were Jarvis Tatum who played for the California Angels, Joe Henderson who played for the Chicago White Sox and Cincinnati, and John Dixon. All were inducted into the Edison High Baseball Hall of Fame in 2010 (Tatum posthumously). Henderson and Dixon credited Aldredge for being someone they respected as he helped their baseball development. Aldredge was Tatum's Big Brother in the Big Brother-Big Sisters program.

If these few athletes (most likely among many others) called Aldredge their hero, one question begs an answer: Who were Aldredge's athletic heroes?

The Rev. Miller supplied the first answer from a seemingly unlikely place: home. It was Aldredge's brother. Indeed, can those so close to us be our "heroes"? Miller emphasized that his brother and other Edison "legends" set powerful examples for Aldredge about competitive toughness. "Jim's big brother, John, was certainly a football legend at Edison. We all called him 'Big Hoss,' and he dominated the line of scrimmage in almost every football game," Miller said. John also excelled at throwing the discus and the shot put.

Two other athletes qualified as Aldredge's heroes: Johnny Morse and Huey Davis.

As early as the fifth grade at Kirk Elementary, Aldredge had heard all about one four-sport standout who competed for Edison High. Play-by-play radio announcers calling Edison's football games extolled his abilities, and adults and kids alike talked about only one athlete above all others: Johnny Morse. His name was still on their tongues three years after he was graduated in 1946.

Morse also was a track star and competed in the West Coast Relays in 1948 when Mel Patton was billed as "the world's fastest human." Patton tied the world record of 9.4 seconds in the 100-yard dash in 1947 and lowered it to 9.3 in 1948. Morse also played basketball at Edison and at Fresno State College when it was possible to be a letterman in several sports. He didn't simply ride the bench. He excelled at every sport he attempted, and that impressed the young Aldredge.

Because Morse left Fresno after college in 1950, playing minor league baseball until 1957 and living in Stockton for many years, the two had never met. In September 2008, Aldredge heard that Morse had returned to Fresno, and arrangements were made for them to meet. At a Mexican café in west Fresno's Chinatown district, Aldredge met his first hero. Morse was as impressed as Aldredge was 60-plus years earlier when he first heard Morse's name. "However," he said, "Jim's reputation preceded him as a great ballplayer and great human being, and it was a pleasure to finally meet him in Fresno over a cup of coffee."

The other athletic hero who preceded Aldredge at Edison was Huey Davis, an outstanding basketball and baseball player. Just as Aldredge was nearing a turning point athletically, he was seeking to elevate himself academically, at age 13. Davis showed him the possibilities. Davis won the B'nai B'rith award in 1953. Aldredge had the goal he had been looking for, and he would "try, try, try and try again, and keep the faith."

With Davis winning the award in 1953, Aldredge winning in 1956 and Miller in 1959—three distinguished student-athletes every three years—they could, indeed, compete with "the big boys."

PART THREE

The Halls of Learning

Chapter Twenty

HE CAN DO IT

The summer after high school, the annual City-County All-Star Classic football game for the Valley was coming up. The game was originated the year before by the Fresno 20-30 Club and, sure, players competed at Ratcliffe Stadium, the home field of the Fresno State Bulldogs, but, being only the second game, it didn't mean as much as it would through the years. Of course the top Valley players were chosen, and Aldredge was one of them. He feared he would get hurt playing football and end his baseball career, so he chose not to play. Ironically, two years later, the eye injury did exactly that.

While waiting to start classes at Fresno City College, he played sandlot baseball, first with the Nisei All-Stars, the local Japanese team that played on the weekends. In the evenings, he played on the Fresno City College Summer League team in the Twilight League. On the nights when he didn't have a game, he swung an extra heavy bat for two or three hours in his back yard to improve his swing and bat speed.

All the playing and all the swings and all the work hoisting hay bales in the field put blisters on the palms of both hands. Not only was he suffering with blisters, but his effectiveness at the plate also suffered. The City College coach, Tom Mockler, couldn't figure it out until Aldredge showed him the blisters. Mockler was stunned. "I had no idea that your hands were in that bad of shape. You have to do lighter and less damaging work than hauling hay." The coach telephoned Paul Starr, an official in the Fresno Unified School District, about a new job for Aldredge. He was hired, and the blisters started to heal and his batting average got healthy.

The City College team won the sectionals and the district title of the American Amateur Baseball Congress and qualified for the Little

World Series in Watertown, S.D. The team finished second in the tournament. Selected to the All-Tournament first team were Aldredge, Kalem Barserian and Al Alanis. Barserian was graduated from Roosevelt High School and transferred his talents to the 1959 Fresno City College championship team, which included Jim Maloney.

When the fall semester began, the Fresno City team played in the Winter League, and Aldredge played that season—until December when he signed with the Pittsburgh Pirates. Meanwhile, he had put one semester of college behind him.

*   *   *

Upon the City College team's return at the start of the fall semester, Aldredge was surprised—and chagrined—to learn that an assistant coach had registered him for classes. Although it was a nice gesture, none of his classes was transferable to a four-year college. He thought it was insensitive at best and uncaring at worst. He immediately dropped every class and re-registered for classes that had more value to him. "After spending my first 17 years focusing on basic survival, basic education, career preparation and personal self-identity, why would I keep classes like techniques of baseball, techniques of football and basket-weaving?" They were irrelevant for a major in business administration.

Aldredge's new schedule included literature, psychology and history and, of course, accounting, marketing and business math. He earned his best grades in zoology, biology and world geography. But typing class? He revealed, jokingly: "I never got past the tremendous speed of 25 words per minute typing, but I passed the class. Maybe I passed because I could spell.

"Having just come to City College out of high school, my success in biology classes, in particular, was a real surprise. Now, I said to myself, 'Gee, with the grace of God, I can do this college work,' because I was sitting alongside students from Fresno High, San Joaquin Memorial High, Roosevelt High and other top-notch students from out of town, and doing quite well. My classmates were certainly not considered academically at-risk students, but rather good college student material, and I was able to compete successfully in all my classes. I was really trying to get good grades in all of my classes because, whenever I was comparing grades with my fellow students, I was right there with them and, in a lot of cases, ahead of them."

Not only did this boost his confidence, but he also came to this realization: "The secret was that you've got to go to the library between classes and study. I thought to myself, 'You can do it.' And I also said to myself, 'Jim, don't be tempted to sit in the cafeteria and "talk stuff" with the guys and girls because if you do, you will have academic problems resulting in academic non-performance very quickly.'"

He also found time to become involved in student government, just as he had at Edison High. At Fresno City, he was the Student Council's commissioner of athletics. He collaborated with Student Council president David Hanna on creating plans for a cooperative program with the YMCA. The idea did not progress beyond the planning stage because Aldredge left for spring training.

*   *   *

Although Aldredge had ultimate success in college, he is not hidebound to a college education for everyone because not everyone is college material. At the same time, he believes that is no excuse for dropping out of high school. "One can always pursue a good vocational or liberal arts education while in high school," he said, "in order to get a job upon graduation from high school. That's a better alternative than dropping out, which disadvantages a person for the rest of his or her life.

"There are many countries in the world that consider education as a privilege for only the privileged class. But in the United States, it is a right. Professional sports aside, I knew that in the United States, education is considered a right of the lower socioeconomic class student, as well as the upper socioeconomic student. People could make something of themselves if they try, notwithstanding issues of ethnicity or *de facto* segregation of students."

He connected an education with business and tried to look ahead as far as possible, whether in baseball or out of baseball.

"I speak from firsthand knowledge that someday a person who has been involved in sports on an amateur or professional basis has to face reality. Whether the participation in sports ends because of an injury like mine, or a person has reached the highest level of his or her ability, all good things must come to an end. The question then is, What do you do? Or better yet, What are you prepared to do?"

The questions are directed at any tall eighth-grade kid who is being recruited by Division I and Division II universities. Those schools' recruiters have him believing he can play in the NBA, but he doesn't have a midget's chance if he doesn't grow another 10 inches.

When his career ended abruptly, Aldredge said, faith, education, knowledge and skills provided him with the ability to deal with the traumatic change in his life. "When an athlete's career is over, he or she often sees others in the spotlight that once was his or hers. As a result, he or she may feel that the new athlete's talent is not even a down payment on what they brought to their particular sport."

He urges amateur and professional athletes to ask themselves early in their careers: "When the lights go out at the stadium or arena, and the crowd leaves, what do you do with your personal life? How will you handle the situation?"

*   *   *

After his eye injury in Lincoln, Aldredge chose to leave his damaged eye just as it was. There would be no prosthetic eye for one reason—he could show young athletes how fragile an eye is and how quickly precious sight can be lost. Of course, the ever-present sunglasses hide the damaged eye—until he takes them off and displays the eye. The shock is effective. The eye is a ghastly blue swirl swimming in a sea of milk.

At home, he was determined to earn an Associate of Arts degree at City College, and simultaneously began work on a bachelor's degree in summer school at Fresno State.

To say he was driven is an understatement. He simply puts it this way: He was testing his prayers, academic speed and ability. Reading with only one eye did not slow him down.

But wearing sunglasses day and night? Wasn't that a little too much? He felt compelled to reveal the reason: "Starting with Fresno City College, I had to explain to all of my college classroom teachers that I had to wear shades in class due to an eye injury and that it was not because I thought it was cool."

Then, there was that first comeback attempt, and his intense progress in college was interrupted by the short-lived comeback with Portland

and then Tri-City in the Kansas City organization in 1959.[13] By leaving Tri-City and returning to Fresno, he thought he could wipe baseball out of his future and resume his education.

Arriving at home, he exchanged warm greetings with his mother. Then, he said, "The first thing I did was call Fresno State College to see about summer school. Education was still important to me and, from then on, I went to school year-round."

Minutes later, he called the Fresno Parks and Recreation Department about becoming a playground leader or umpiring again. That busy day was also the day he wrote his resignation from baseball to the Tri-City team and included his mailing address so the team could mail his final paycheck. He thought he had gotten baseball out of his system.

Within two weeks, he was convinced even more. He was blessed to be hired as a playground leader and as an umpire for the City of Fresno. He also finished lining up classes for his undergraduate major, minor and elective courses at Fresno State. In the fall, he returned to City College to complete an Associate of Arts degree in business administration.

"Reaping the benefits of a solid education has always been a work in progress, and I didn't plan to deviate from my philosophy of lifelong learning," Aldredge said.

"Every human being seeks to be significant in one way or another. Sports activity, as such, often provides this feedback of personal significance. However, for some people, their sports performance could be considered a personal failure because a certain athletic goal was not reached. An education can help in the complete success of an athlete."

---

[13] By mutual agreement, the Pirates had given him his outright release, and he was free to sign with another team.

Chapter Twenty-One

HEAVY SCHEDULES

For the Aldredges, education and work were always inseparable. You couldn't have one without the other.

By 1959, his mother's divorce was final, and she was free to pursue her lifelong dream. Knowing how much she emphasized education, it is not surprising that her dream was to resume the education that came to a halt after the ninth grade, 40-plus years earlier. Wanting to become a licensed vocational nurse, she enrolled at Fresno Adult School for one year. It proved to be the wrong profession because varicose veins made it too painful for her to stand for long periods of times.

But the work she faced was more difficult than cleaning houses during the week and chopping cotton on the weekends. In the divorce settlement, she was awarded two substandard rental houses, and they needed constant maintenance. Mrs. Aldredge would tackle some of it, for example, painting only the lower half of the walls because the pain in her legs prevented her from standing on a ladder. When Aldredge came home from school or work, he would paint the top part of the walls.

*   *   *

Aldredge somehow found the time and energy despite a packed schedule—homework, classes at City College and Fresno State, half-day shifts on the playground, volunteering as an official at high school track and field meets, and at the famous West Coast Relays at Ratcliffe Stadium. He umpired baseball and softball games, including women's softball games featuring the Fresno Rockets, who had won the World

Amateur Softball Association championships in 1953, 1954 and 1957.[14] Aldredge fondly remembers the Rockets' victory parade along Van Ness Avenue after their championship in 1957. "When I look back at it, it was a blessing to get the opportunity to umpire world-class women's softball games, featuring a team right here in Fresno that was before its time."

His inspiration to umpire came after he watched Vernon Riggins umpire women's games. They eventually officiated games together, and Aldredge umpired men's fast-pitch games, featuring Leroy Zimmerman, who was one of the great pitchers of his time, and Max Downs, another outstanding pitcher who later became Fresno's police chief.

"Can you imagine a guy with one good eye umpiring behind the plate in baseball or softball, and timing runners at the finish line in a track meet? Well, I did it, and nobody complained." There were photo finishes in track in the days of hand-held stop watches. Nobody protested or overturned his calls. If the softball spectators had known it, they may have used the familiar taunt: "He's blind in one eye, and can't see out of the other."

School and playground work obligations did interrupt his officiating duties, and a six-week-long hiatus ultimately led to his cutting out officiating. As an official, he was quite aware that a missed call here and there happens. While umpiring a top-flight women's regional softball tournament, he missed a call during a routine double play, and it ended up affecting the outcome of the game. Umpires always know when they make a mistake, but rarely do they admit it affected a win. In Aldredge's mind, there was no doubt, and he admitted to himself that he was not as sharp as he should be, or in the best condition. He decided then to retire from umpiring and refereeing.

"Umpires are human, and they all make mistakes. However, you just cannot go into a game knowing beforehand that you are capable of making a game-changing mistake because you have not called enough games to be sharp and be on your game. That type of missed call is more

---

[14] The Rockets were led by five-time national tournament All-Star Jeanne Contel at third base and fellow All-Stars Kay Rich at shortstop, Theresa Urrutia of Edison High School at second base, Yvonne Clausen in centerfield, Gloria May at first base, Betsy Schlegel at catcher, and pitchers Joan Alsup, Carole Nelson and Virginia Busick.

understandable at the beginning of the season, but not in late-season playoffs and championships."

Aldredge tied all of his officiating experiences together by writing a manual for baseball, basketball, football and soccer officials in Fresno's recreational leagues. Some high school and college officials used the manual as well, when they graduated from the recreational leagues.

Through his years of officiating, he learned that he would need to have unyielding courage and commitment if he expected it from those who worked with him.

* * *

While working at home was difficult and working as an LVN impossible, his mother refused to be discouraged. She simply found something else to do. She joined her son and enrolled at Fresno City College in 1959.

"She then became even more of a rooting section and fan," Aldredge said, "as I completed my educational goals during my last semester at City College. I was so proud that we were on the same campus at the same time and getting a chance to get a college-level education." Being fellow students also reinforced to them that they would continue to demonstrate the application of God's grace on their life's journey for advancement through education. Her enrolling also eased some of the pain of not being able to complete school as a young lady in Gilmer, Texas. Aldredge said: "My grandmother's refusal to grant my mother her educational opportunity haunted her until her death at the age of 86."

* * *

For the next three years, he worked his full schedule for the Recreation Department and continued his year-round college schedule. It was 1962, and he was 22. Then the irresistible call came for the tryout in Salinas. This time, the interruption was only a blip of four days. He knew baseball was over for good this time, and he quickly was back on track to graduate from Fresno State in 1964.

Declaring a double minor in sociology and psychology, he set out to graduate in therapeutic recreation with the goal of working in Veterans Administration hospitals. As if his schedule wasn't full enough, he also was interning as a recreation therapist at the Fresno Veterans hospital. And with a dearth of academic scholarships at that time, Aldredge still had to earn money—working when and where he could, again in the fields on large west-side farms, just as he had done during middle school and high school.

He wasn't alone, and childhood friend Dr. Felton Burns described the time:

"Jim and I had to work like crazy when we started going to Fresno State. There were hardly any academic scholarships available. There were no work-study programs. So student employees on campus, like Jim's part-time job in the Fresno State Art Department, were few and far between.

"But Jim and I did what we had to do. Even when we were going to Fresno State, we worked in the fields at tasks such as hauling cantaloupes and watermelons, and hauling hay, to further supplement our incomes."

Aldredge did find the part-time job in the Art Department. He developed photographic film, enlarged photos, hung art exhibits and—his favorite task—shooting artists' animations for cartoons. It was one of three jobs he held simultaneously. For the city, he had been assigned as an assistant playground supervisor as a part of an internship in his major at Fresno State.

"Few people ever found out about my Art Department job. It wasn't a case of me being ashamed of it as a macho athlete. I photographed the cartoon characters and took all the still drawings and photographs, and developed them for my supervisor, Professor Ella Ordorfer. I also enjoyed hanging all of the hall and gallery art exhibits throughout the whole college. That was a great experience that sometimes extended my work schedule to well over 60 hours a week."

He described himself simply as "the guy up on the ladder with Mrs. Ordorfer spotting the pictures, and so I learned a lot about balance. I'm talking about balance in terms of where you put the pictures and light reflections and all the rest of the art gallery and museum stuff."

Chapter Twenty-Two

AN INTERLUDE

Naïve America of the 1950s stubbornly resisted admitting that the seemingly disparate worlds of baseball and alcoholism, baseball and racism, baseball and pressure existed cheek by jowl. And certainly speaking of lowbrow baseball and the highbrow world of arts in the same sentence was like fingernails on a blackboard. Author and playwright James Baldwin thought otherwise.

In the summer of 1968, Baldwin had come to Fresno to dig deeply into the deleterious effects alcoholism, racism and pressure had on the black baseball player. His quest was to write a book, a play, a movie script, telling some tragic stories. He named his project "Rough Diamond," and he sought the help of Jim Aldredge.

Aldredge laughs and says that his brief brush with the arts qualified him—possibly—to work with Baldwin on his project.

For Baldwin, it was important to know that Aldredge had tasted racism in baseball and had grown up watching an alcoholic father. Even more important, Aldredge knew Hank Thompson, the star third baseman for the New York Giants in the 1951 and 1954 World Series.

The challenges Thompson faced in his life were extraordinary. The peaks were incredible, and the valleys were unimaginable. He was a decorated machine-gunner in the Battle of the Bulge in World War II. He was the third black player in the major leagues after Jackie Robinson and Larry Doby. He batted .364 against the Cleveland Indians in the '54 World Series. Throughout his years with the Giants, manager Leo Durocher kept warning Thompson about his drinking and, by 1956, he was sent down to the minors, his talents eroding precipitously. When he couldn't catch a routine fly ball, he was so embarrassed that he quit baseball in the middle of the season. From the beginning of his life to the end, he was in and out of reform school and jail, committing stickups usually when he was drunk. But there were those nine excellent years with the Giants when he was their anchor at third base.

Long after baseball, Thompson moved to Fresno to be near his mother, and he met Betty Turner and married her in 1968.

Aldredge knew the Turner sisters from their elementary school days at Fresno Colony, and Thompson was hired to be a leader at Frank H. Ball Playground. That job lasted awhile, and then Thompson was off to seek a dream job in baseball. But soon, he returned and suffered a seizure in September 1969. He died at the Fresno Veterans Hospital at age 43.

But, in 1968, Aldredge provided technical assistance on Baldwin's project. Again, his focus was on the ups and downs of black players and how they coped with pressure outside the haven of the two Negro Leagues, which, for all intents and purposes, met their demise after the 1951 season. His plan was to dissect Thompson's inability to endure the pressures at baseball's highest level amid race and social issues in New York City.

Aldredge said Thompson's problems were exacerbated by the daily pressure on African-American players in the major leagues. "Pressure," he told Baldwin, "it was and is real."

Upon reflection decades later, Aldredge allowed that perhaps his father's alcoholism could be traced to social and economic pressures of the "Promised Land" after World War II—pressures so great that they could result in a man like his father or a player like Thompson drinking himself to an early death.

Aldredge told Baldwin his father's story along with what it was like to take racial insults as a player. "In short," Aldredge said, "those nine baseball team starting spots were much like Jim Crow hotel rooms. If you were colored, most of those positions had no vacancies."

Aldredge sat in on many sessions with Baldwin and Thompson discussing baseball, discrimination in society and pressures faced by athletes of color.

Baldwin interrupted work on the "Rough Diamond" project in Fresno so that he could go home to Paris and take care of some personal business. Unfortunately, he died in France on December 1, 1987, and the "Rough Diamond" project was never finished.

PART FOUR

The Career Years

Chapter Twenty-Three

THE VOLATILE SIXTIES

After graduation from Fresno State, Aldredge was hired as a program developer for the Fresno County Economic Opportunity Commission in the War on Poverty.[15] He was the second administrative staff member hired in late 1964 when the agency was created. Its director was John Lindberg.

The job mirrored Aldredge's philosophy of spreading as much good fortune as he could to those with only misfortune.

He helped to start Project 17 (it has been renamed to Upward Bound), and there was a young girl, Dorothy "Dottie" Smith, who had recently graduated from Washington Union High School at age 17 in 1967. The project helped to send her on a path to a successful, 37-year career as an English teacher, middle school principal and counselor. She said Project 17 played an integral role in her rise out of poverty. Forty-two years later, it was Smith who introduced Aldredge as an inductee for Fresno City College's Community Service Wall of Fame, and she added a personal highlight: "Jim saw something in me and other young minority students that we did not know was there ourselves."

*   *   *

But three years earlier, Aldredge was only months removed from Fresno State, and how could he know that the War on Poverty would

---

[15]   The War on Poverty was President Lyndon B. Johnson's response in 1964 to a soaring national rate of poverty. Legislation created the Economic Opportunity Act and the Office of Economic Opportunity.

spark an international brouhaha in the other war at the time—the Cold War between the United States and the Soviet Union—all the way from Moscow to Cantua Creek in west Fresno County? The flap would encompass journalism, international relations, views of class struggles and improving farmworker housing.

In 1965, his primary territory was west Fresno County, and he was in charge of five staff members with the Volunteers in Service to America. (VISTA became AmeriCorps.) Three of them were based at the North Avenue Community Center in west Fresno and two in Parlier.

Seeking to use world public opinion against the United States, the Kremlin sent Pravda newspaper reporters in search of damning examples of capitalism (the bourgeoisie) vs. the working class (the proletariat). They wrote in-depth stories alleging exploitation of Mexican farmworkers employed by white farmers. The reports focused on tiny Three Rocks in the heart of America's richest agricultural region and exposed insufferable living conditions.

Pravda's articles caught the attention of Sargent Shriver, the director of the Office of Economic Opportunity. He sent the articles and letters to Lindberg and asked him to handle the situation as pragmatically as possible. He would take care of the politics.

Shriver was particularly galled at the Pravda articles because he was one of the world's most famous Democratic politicians and humanitarians. (He was part of the Kennedy family by way of his marriage to Eunice Kennedy.)

Aldredge realized, with two colossal governments standing toe to toe, that the sparring was nearing an all-out slugfest, as the main mouthpiece of the Soviet Union and the Communist Party kept popping off. That meant he was dealing with the heaviest of international heavyweights as the man in charge of improving the living and housing conditions for farmworkers in Three Rocks.

Using the core principles taught to him by his mother—to fear only God and her, Aldredge exposed Pravda's inaccuracies while helping farmworker children at Cantua Creek Elementary School. "They say if you can't run with the big dogs, don't get off of the porch," he said. "And I had been off the porch for as far back as I could remember." A Head Start program already was in place. He also helped to initiate self-help housing with people contributing "sweat-equity" labor and building their own houses.

"Mr. Tom Zavala came on board with Fresno County EOC," Aldredge said, "and established Self-Help Enterprises. Zavala was a licensed general contractor. The federal government paid for the construction supervision while the potential homeowner put in the sweat equity to build a group of 10 houses simultaneously."

Pravda stories continued to blast the U.S. government and farmers on the county's west side. But, in about 18 months, all 10 houses were built, and the program continued to be a success in Three Rocks. Three more successful phases followed, and Sargent Shriver and the federal government were generally pleased with the self-help subdivisions.

*   *   *

Although international strife in Fresno's back yard was fleeting, its arrival coincided with other turbulent issues rapidly gaining momentum as the decade of the volatile 1960s began: The Civil Rights Movement. Race riots in the Watts area of Los Angeles. The Black Power Movement in Oakland. The Free Speech Movement in Berkeley. The United Farm Workers' grape strike in Delano. Indeed, Fresno soon would catch, first hand, the meaning of the lyrics of "The Times Are a-Changin'."

In 1966, as a deputy city manager, Aldredge was appointed the city's first director of Human Relations. He came along at the right time in the city's history.

With disenfranchised residents specifically in mind, he believed that, in order to make changes in the public interest, people like himself must be at the table where decisions are made and policies are shaped on public, economic and social direction.

More to the point, the job was created to combat the hidden and obvious outward discrimination in Fresno, which had oppressed long-established residents from Armenians in central Fresno to the African-American ghetto to the Mexican-American barrio in west and southeast Fresno. These ethnic minority neighborhoods were generally south of Belmont Avenue, which runs east and west through the city. Aldredge alternately refers to Belmont Avenue in the 1960s as the city's "have and have-not's line" and as Fresno's Mason-Dixon Line. Either way, it was the city's great divide of race and affluence.

Aldredge faced all imaginable problems: fights over discrimination in housing, employment and *de facto* segregation in the Fresno Unified

School District. Racism was part and parcel of the implied warnings he heard about his new post:

Do a good job and he was favoring racial minorities, and would be fired. Do a poor job and he was neglecting minorities, and would be fired. Detractors and supporters told him that he would not last more than two years on the job. He was in a quandary.

The naysayers did not know that Aldredge had grown up with a father who could spew venom mercilessly. Or the racism he faced as a professional baseball player. Or his days of dealing with hateful, racist kids in Calwa. He considered questions about his human relations knowledge and skills as lightweight.

He would be tested again soon.

*   *   *

The nascent UFW held its first national conference at Selland Arena in Fresno on March 11, 1966, and the city knew it had to accommodate the strikers and to keep worried farmers calm.

Aldredge's solution provided free space at city-run gymnasiums for sleeping, restrooms and shower facilities. He and the 15-member Human Relations Commission respected the strikers, regardless of the politics of the grape strike.

Less than one week later, March 17, 1966, strikers left Delano and began a city-to-city, 300-mile march up the middle of the Central Valley on their way to Sacramento to protest their low wages. They stopped in Fresno overnight, and the city provided for them again.

The next test was on Oct. 22, 1966, when Sen. Robert F. Kennedy spoke in front of 10,000 people in the city's Roeding Park. Aldredge was there and heard Kennedy say, "California can provide the leadership for solving the problems of civil rights, poverty and education for all. California stands for the concept that things can be better."[16]

It was a moving scene, Aldredge said. "He didn't have to sell me on anything because I already liked the Kennedy family and what they stood for." He also said, "I think people had mixed feelings about Robert Kennedy." Kennedy supported desegregation. "The more conservative folks didn't like it."

---

[16] Quoted in The Fresno Bee, June 5, 2008.

*   *   *

Protests on college campuses and in cities—including anti-Vietnam War demonstrations—had been building since 1964, and, in 1966, the unrest spread to the West Coast Relays, one of the world's premier track and field meets. When bigger protests hit the University of California campus in Berkeley in 1967, Gov. Ronald Reagan cancelled the international event in Fresno.

The year before, Fresno got a bad taste of civil disobedience when revelers from the track meet went overboard and caused damage at hotels, motels and restaurants. The city knew it had to come up with a solution if the Relays were going to resume in 1968. Besides, it was an Olympic year.

Aldredge told the Human Relations Commission and the Fresno City Council that he had a workable solution. Today, he jokes and says, "Tailgating started at the West Coast Relays in Fresno." He recommended modifying a city ordinance that would allow all-night dancing at three downtown hotels with liquor service stopping at 3:30 a.m. Dance bands could play until sunrise. Nearby Roeding Park also stayed open all night. The solution worked, the Relays resumed and track fans, merchants and residents were happy.

His success in the UFW and West Coast Relays problems was attributed to his humility and wisdom to recognize the tensions of the times between all races. It has been said that he also did not bring a heavy hand when he presented his solutions.

"Jim was always a problem solver," said Kathy Millison, the city manager in Santa Rosa in 2013. They knew each other from the days when she worked for the Clovis city manager. "While working with Jim when he was at Fresno City Hall, he was always a person that would come to the table and say, 'OK, you know, let's see what kind of problem we have here and find a solution that can be win-win.'"

*   *   *

Folded in with all of Aldredge's studying, projects and problem-solving, he found time to use his talents as Fresno's first African-American television host on a network affiliate. From 1967 to 1971, he teamed with Al Geller as co-hosts of a weekly program about community issues. It was called "Opportunity Line." More specifically, the two tackled such issues as education, discrimination and employment in Fresno and the Central Valley. Aldredge later became the single host of a PBS program titled "Crime: the Impact." He knew that he would have to use all his skills and be twice as good as competitors in the Fresno market in order to draw a sustaining viewer base.

*   *   *

It was still 1966 when Aldredge was appointed a deputy city manager for Fresno and in charge of the Model Cities Program, sponsored by the U.S. Department of Housing and Urban Development. He was 29 years old.

Aldredge and colleague Walt Slipe prepared the HUD application for the high poverty area of west Fresno, which encompassed approximately 28,000 people. Fresno's application went a step beyond the Human Relations Commission's intergroup activity of overt discrimination to more tangible programs for better housing, employment, improved health facilities and better education.

Fresno Mayor Floyd Hyde (who became undersecretary of HUD and directed the national Model Cities program) was a key ally of Aldredge's.

Chapter Twenty-Four

SOMEBODY'S ALWAYS UNHAPPY

Since childhood, Aldredge had been fighting a personal war on poverty. Now that he was in a position of authority, he sought to expand his war to the poor and needy in west Fresno. He called it "domestic foreign aid."

Subsequently, federal funds flowed to Fresno's Model Cities Program during the War on Poverty as long as it showed positive results in its five-year duration.

Aldredge, Slipe and Hyde used Model Cities money on such west Fresno projects as the long-awaited Ivy Neighborhood Center (it replaced the North Avenue Community Center) and a swimming pool in the west Fresno area. Homes with swimming pools did not exist in west Fresno, and the only choices were irrigation ditches.

The scope of such an accomplishment transcended the ins and outs of bureaucracy, and west Fresno residents must have jumped with joy about the center—with a measure of patience. The Fresno Bee reported on October 30, 1972: "It will be years before the ivy is clinging to the walls of the center, but at long last the Ivy Community Center in southwest Fresno is under way."[17]

*   *   *

Aldredge's time as head of Model Cities was during the spike in minority hiring in white-collar jobs. Until then, most jobs were available only in agriculture. Unions were hesitant to hire minorities. Aldredge's

---

[17]   Quoted in a story by reporter Edwin M. Clough.

philosophy about the Model Cities program in Fresno was that "the rising tide lifts all boats" and domestic aid was needed.

Aldredge was proud of the progress that the city was making with teacher training and certification, police and firefighter recruitment, and other staff training programs for more ethnic minorities.

But some people were not satisfied.

The Rev. Harry Miller said, "Of course, there were some blacks who, if they did not get everything they wanted, complained that Jim was doing too much for whites or too much for Hispanics, or both."

Aldredge readily admitted that those feelings existed among some blacks, but he knew that Fresno was a diverse city of 85 or more different ethnic groups and a population of more than 166,000 people—rich and poor alike, and he was determined to serve everyone, especially those in need of better housing, health services and education.

The Model Cities program included the Minority Teacher Certification program. One pointed example of the success of the rising-tide philosophy is the Rev. Jim Parks, once a postal worker who went on to earn a law degree at Harvard University. Parks specialized in workers' compensation cases until he became a full-time pastor at the West Fresno Christian Church in 2008.

Parks told how Aldredge served with a low profile and humility. "I never knew Jim was involved with the teacher-credentialing program, and it has been 40 years now. And if it was left up to him, I probably never would have found out." He learned that fact from Dolphus Trotter, who was the superintendent of the West Fresno School District before he died of cancer in 2009.

"Jim never wavered from his belief that education should, and must, be the cornerstone for improving the lives of the so-called 'have-nots' in our society," Trotter said.

Aldredge, his city staff and HUD Undersecretary Hyde also worked on One Reach One, which featured junior high and senior high school students tutoring younger students. The program was a modification of the Laubach reading method used in the Philippines to improve that country's literacy rate.

Still more positives were realized when Model Cities joined forces with the Chamber of Commerce to establish the YES program, as in Youth Education Scholarships. Aldredge is proud that the YES program used private funding and, with help from the Chamber's then-Executive

Director Russ Sloan, distributed gift certificates to young people who were identified as being at risk of dropping out of school.

Aldredge said, "Nonetheless, they were students who we felt had the ability to stay in school if they were given the encouragement to succeed. Along those lines, the gift certificates, for example, were immediate, and what I like to call 'short-term encouragers.'"

With all this success, Aldredge, at age 32, was promoted to assistant city manager in 1971 by City Administrative Officer Bruce Reiss. Aldredge was in charge of all federal and state programs in the city.

About the same time, the five-year Model Cities program was coming to an end and, with it, the YES program also expired. As Model Cities was closing down, Aldredge reorganized Fresno's Parks and Recreation Department, adding a community services division for social service programs for all the ethnic groups in town.

Chapter Twenty-Five

THE CLASSROOM BECKONS

For Aldredge, the subject of education was never far off, and a new door suddenly opened leading back to the classroom, first as an instructor and again as a student. The head of the Criminology Department at Fresno State College let him know that he was welcome to teach a class in human relations as a part-time, adjunct faculty member, and he learned that a master's degree would be required to teach at a community college and eventually a doctorate at a university.

1969 marked the start of nearly 40 years of teaching at the college level and his quest for postgraduate degrees.

True to form, all of this was a part of his need to have a plan in place—his obsession since 8 or 9 years old—when his municipal career was over. He reminded himself that he could do this—with God's grace. So he began post-graduate studies and earned a master's degree in public administration in 1976 from Fresno State University.

Some of his fellow students in his master's degree classes were people who worked for him at Fresno's City Hall. "I couldn't afford to have an ego saying, 'I'm too good for them,' if I wanted to make it to my desired goal of earning a master's degree on my way to being able to teach at the college and university level." Having a thought like that would be disingenuous.

Meanwhile, he was promoted to assistant city manager in charge of labor relations, budgets and the departments of fire, police, parks and community service.

Not long after, he began work toward a doctoral degree. That journey would start at the University of Southern California campus in Sacramento with intense, eight-hour classes Friday-through-Monday every six weeks. It would wend its way to Golden Gate University of San Francisco, with a stop in Oxford, England.

Accumulated vacation time was more than enough to allow him to attend classes. "I didn't tell anyone at City Hall about USC because I knew how some of my fellow bureaucrats were. So, it was again, if they don't ask, then I don't tell." He said his studies never affected his job at City Hall negatively.

However, in February 1974, his boss, City Manager Ralph Hanley, told him that he was needed in the office every day. Hanley said that being out of town on Fridays and Mondays was not going to work anymore because of his budget and labor relations responsibilities, especially during the spring semester.

"I was not sure that was the real reason for Ralph Hanley not allowing me to go to school once every six weeks. After all, I was using my accumulated vacation time, which actually came out to only four workdays every two months. And I paid for every dime of the USC program out of my own pocket, and all the while I was working well over 10 to 12 hours a day and many times on Saturdays. Once again, I relied on my faith in God's grace and continued to do everything in my power to find another alternative in my quest for a doctorate degree so that I would only be sidetracked temporarily."

The need for him to have even more faith was right around the corner.

Chapter Twenty-Six

ALL-NIGHT PRAYER

Aldredge said, "One of the last classes that I took at USC before the Hanley order was Statistics and Research, and that was the hardest course that I had ever taken in my entire college career."

The difficult class and his boss' order were challenging pressures. Aldredge described the situation:

"I could not understand anything that my statistics professor wrote on the blackboard, nor could I make either head or tail of the data in our textbook. This caused me to second-guess myself and concede that there was no way that I could pass the class.

"The professor was named Dr. Holman, and he was one of the most renowned statistics instructors in the United States. We had a number of formulas and words like Molotov Z and T tests and that kind of statistical language. Throughout the entire first day, all of my classmates seemed to understand all the formulas and concepts, but I didn't."

For a few minutes, Aldredge felt that the devil had him in his grip, squeezing thoughts out of his inner self that, up to then, had been virtually unthinkable for him.

"I said to myself, 'I cannot do this stuff. I can't remember these formulas. There are too many of them. So, I guess I'll finish this weekend, and this is probably going to be the end of my doctorate hopes. Or I've got to figure something else out because this is a required class.' A required class that, to me, was like three foreign languages.

"When the first class was over, I decided to go heavy to God after recalling the epiphany I had at the Mets' training camp in Salinas and a full night of prayer that led to me deciding to end my baseball career.

"So I went back to my motel room, and, praying similar to what I understand to be like Jacob wrestling with the angel,[18] I said, 'God, I really need you to help me on this,' because I knew it would take divine intervention to survive that class." He asked God to grant him the memory or "something" to deal with the statistical formulas. Neither Jacob nor Aldredge let the angel go, and he prayed all night except for a nap from about 5 a.m. until 7 a.m. when his alarm clock awoke him for his second day of class.

Later that morning, a miracle occurred.

The professor announced that, after reassessing the work he was teaching and assigning to each student, he had decided to change his approach.

The change was philosophical as well as practical, and it materialized in the form of the course being tailored to the students' professional needs. Dr. Holman decided it was more important for them to learn to read statistical research reports and know what practical concepts they were being taught. Consequently, the students would be better equipped to apply these statistical formulas and concepts to their professions, like in Aldredge's case, city administration.

All the formulas that had baffled Aldredge on the first day were unnecessary. His reaction: "Oh, my goodness, God has answered my prayer, and you know what? I know now I can do this."

As the class continued, his grasp of the complex material became easier.

By persevering through God to escape a rare surrender to self-doubt and wavering confidence, Aldredge left the Sacramento campus that Monday on a positive note, "giving thanks to God again and again" all the way home from Sacramento to Fresno, 170 miles to the south.

He said that after the first day of class, "I was dead in the water, but God's grace had made the second day of the doctorate statistics a major part of the first day of the rest of my life. It was a perfect—and God-given—rite of passage and a new beginning. The homework given for the next session in six weeks related to applied statistical methods rather than the theoretical formulas.

"The load was lighter, the prayer was answered, and, as I read more material on the subject of statistics, I vowed not to ever cheat myself by

---

[18]   Genesis 32:22-32.

not having faith in God. For, once again, I knew, by the grace of God, 'I can do all things through Christ who strengthens me.'[19] He did it before, He did it now and He can do it again."

When Dr. Holman passed out the homework papers after the third day of the four-day intensive weekend, Aldredge's grade was an "A" with this comment attached: "This was one of the best statistics and research papers that I have ever seen in my entire teaching career." It was signed: "Professor Holman." Fittingly, Aldredge "gave God the 'A.'"

---

[19]   Philippians 4:13.

Chapter Twenty-Seven

TRANSFER APPROVED

After being pushed by City Manager Hanley to withdraw from USC so that he could do more in his day job, Aldredge, true to his faith, said, "I knew there was nothing else to do than be part of a complex solution and not the problem as such. With sincere prayer, I chose to, 'Let go and let God.'"

When the statistics course at USC ended, Aldredge started to collect information about transferring to Golden Gate University, given his boss' edict. To his delight, unlike USC, Golden Gate's intensive classes were held on Saturdays and Sundays, with no all-day Fridays and Mondays. And Golden Gate's classes were once every three weeks.

During the transfer to Golden Gate, Aldredge called on the dean of the Public Administration Doctoral Program, Randy Hamilton. They became acquainted when Hamilton worked for the League of California Cities and Aldredge was part of Fresno's successful campaign in Look magazine's All-American City competition. Fresno was awarded the honor for citizen involvement in solving problems in the community. The victory was noted in the issue of April 16, 1968.

Honoring Aldredge's request, Hamilton allowed the transfer of all his classes to Golden Gate. "In addition," Aldredge said, "I found out that many of the classes at Golden Gate were actually tougher than those at USC."

Even with his work schedule, Aldredge was confident he could successfully complete the doctoral course. And he had time to squeeze in a 2½-month independent study course in urban planning at Oxford University in summer 1976. Golden Gate's Hamilton also accepted his grades at Oxford.

"Oxford was a tough one," he recalled. "The classes were taught in small seminars of four to six students by a faculty member called an 'Oxford Don.' In class, you were assigned to lead presentations. You also had to participate constructively in all small-group class seminar discussions and on an assigned basis, while the professor (the Oxford Don) was looking over your shoulder. You've got to perform, so you prepare for class by doing a lot of reading and research." The classroom hours at Oxford were two weeks on campus.

After passing the class at Oxford and returning to Fresno, Aldredge was fiercely determined to complete his doctorate at Golden Gate University with flying colors.

Then, he was slowed, if only briefly, by his mother's interest in a troubling distraction. The Rev. Jim Jones and his People's Temple Church had come to town.

*   *   *

One weekend in the fall of 1976, two Scenicruiser buses pulled up at the curb in front of the Franklin Elementary School, across the street from the Aldredge house, and dozens of acolytes of the People's Temple Church, founded by Jones, piled out.

Mrs. Aldredge and some of her church friends were attracted to the People's Temple Church, and she welcomed them into her back yard as a rest stop on their way from San Francisco to other temples in Los Angeles. For six or seven months, Jones' convoy of buses arrived on their stopovers.

This time, they had descended on Fresno to march around the County Courthouse in support of "The Fresno Bee Four." Fresno Bee Managing Editor George Gruner[20] and Joe Rosato, Jim Patterson and Jim Bort were receiving national attention for being sentenced to indefinite jail sentences by Fresno County Superior Court Judge Hollis Best because they would not divulge confidential sources in a Bee news story.

The Fresno Four were released after spending 15 days in jail.

---

[20] Gruner retired as executive editor of The Bee in 1989. He was 85 years old when he was interviewed for this book in 2010.

"Following our release from jail," Gruner recalled, "we were invited by Jim Jones and the congregation up there to visit them in San Francisco, and we went up there and took part in a regular service at the church. Everybody was really nice to us there, and we expressed our gratitude for their support, and that was our only contact with them. We were in custody at the time that they were marching in support of us, so the only thing that we saw of that demonstration was out the window of the Courthouse building when we appeared before Judge Best. We were completely surprised to see that kind of turnout. We had no background on the group at the time, but we were very grateful for that indication of support."

Unlike Gruner who only attended one service at the People's Temple, Mrs. Aldredge rode Jones' big buses to temples in Los Angeles twice and San Francisco twice.

While her church sisters from places like Fowler and Madera became totally enamored of Jones, Mrs. Aldredge became wary as she witnessed senior citizens being physically abused by Jones with two or three swats during what she said Jones called "discipline."

A few years before, in 1970, Jones had started constructing a model communist community, named Jonestown, in Guyana, South America, and he was quoted, saying, "I believe we're the purest communists there are."

Jones also established social programs in San Francisco, and the idea of more senior citizen programs attracted Mrs. Aldredge. She told Aldredge that Jones was trying to take care of the needy population.

"James," she said, "I would like to give my china cabinet to them." He said fine but explained to her very carefully that Jones' premise of service to the needy was faulty.

After he realized that his mother was politely disagreeing with her son in silence about the impracticality of Jones' proposed programs, he recalled, "I resorted to a rare bass-in-my-voice talk with my rock and inspiration. I looked her in the eye and said, 'Let me tell you something. I run senior citizen programs, which are under my direction as head of Model Cities. You can't run the kind of program that Reverend Jones is proposing with his low, fixed-income membership and community donations. Mother, look me in the eye. I run the Fresno Model Cities program. What Jim Jones is proposing won't work. Do you understand? It won't work.'"

After a moment of reflection that seemed like an hour to him, she said, "James, you are right. One thing I don't like is the discipline of little old ladies. I won't go up there anymore."

Her friends continued to go, and then they stopped coming through Fresno a month or so before November 18, 1978. That was the day Jones' socialist paradise became a suicidal hellhole when 909 inhabitants of Jonestown, including 303 children, followed his orders and swallowed a cyanide-laced drink.

The day before, five people, including U.S. Representative Leo Ryan of San Francisco, were massacred as they were leaving Guyana after a fact-finding mission.

Not only Gruner, but also the entire world watching Jones was shocked by the heinous acts.

Aldredge said, "We never tried to find out exactly who the locals were who got killed. That would have been too tough on my mother. But we knew that some were from this area. When I told her of the deaths, my mother had already heard, but she was strong. She did not cry or show emotion. She was a tough lady. She took it matter-of-factly."

Aldredge summed up the whole difference between Fresno and Jonestown, Guyana: "Let me emphasize, Jones *preyed* not *prayed*, on the poor and dependent people, especially old folks, to set up his proposed Utopia. What they ended up with once they got there were guards on horseback dispensing Jones' twisted brand of social justice and self-help."

*   *   *

With his mother safely out of Jones' influence, Aldredge could concentrate again on his transfer to Golden Gate University. He needed some basic courses to complete the transfer, and he had to double up on classes. Two of those courses were at Golden Gate's campus at Vandenberg Air Force Base.

While driving to class during the fall semester, he often had to navigate his way through thick fog and two-lane highways to Vandenberg, about 240 miles from Fresno.

About 3:30 in the morning one Saturday, Aldredge's car broke down, and he missed class. Missing one class on a weekend of intensive study was comparable to missing two weeks of class on a regular schedule.

"After the morning that I got stranded and couldn't get there," Aldredge said, "the professor worked with me in terms of giving me extra homework and an oral presentation to make up for the seat time I had missed. If not for that professor's accommodations, I would really have messed up my schedule to complete those mandatory transfer courses.

"That car stopping helped me with some attendance policies that I later used in my own classes. You know, taking whatever experiences that you have, looking at them, and if they are positive or bad experiences, they ought to lead to something positive in your instructional career.

"My philosophy with my students became one of advising them never to rush in the fog or bad weather. We had students taking our undergraduate and graduate classes at Fresno State who were commuting to Fresno from 50 to 60 or more miles away for weekend or all-day or weeknight classes when the fog in the San Joaquin Valley, especially in the winter, can really get bad. In many instances, it is difficult to see more than 100 feet in front of you.

"I developed a policy of telling my students if they are late to class or have to miss a class, and they tell me it is because of the bad weather, it's really OK because we are all adults."

On the other hand, he said that if they used bad weather as an excuse to miss the class, they were playing a game on themselves, not him.

"It really is shooting yourself in the foot because, for more than 25 years or so, I always told my students to bring their education buckets to class, and we'll fill them up in here with good usable information. The things that we talk about in here are so good that you'll be missing out on something that is a key career-building component if you don't come.

"I really felt that way about my classes. And the positive comments I get from students that see me after more than three decades verify the notion that my semi-tough-love approach was OK."

*   *   *

His doctoral mission was accomplished in 1984 when he received a Ph.D. in public administration with a specialty in organization development.

He is equally proud that he financed all of his graduate and undergraduate degrees.

"I want to reiterate that all of that studying that I did for my doctorate on weekends and the time that I studied at the University of Southern California, as well as the Fresno City College and Fresno State degrees, were all paid for out of my own pocket."

All the while Aldredge was working for the city, he was teaching classes at Fresno City College, Fresno State (by then with university status), University of San Francisco, National University and Golden Gate University.

PART FIVE

The Years at City Hall

Chapter Twenty-Eight

A TIME OF SURVIVAL

With a doctorate degree in hand at last, Aldredge could look back and smile. It had taken him 14 years. Along the way, he had survived the difficult years under City Manager Ralph Hanley and, in fact, had outlasted Hanley who was fired by the City Council in 1978.

Far in the past were the politics of minor league baseball and, in the not-so-distant past, the sniping politics of municipal government. More were to come.

The council appointed Aldredge interim city manager, the first African-American to hold the position in Fresno.

1978 was the year of Proposition 13[21], and he helped to put the tax amendment into action in Fresno. He immediately faced the challenge of slicing the city's budget because of the greatly reduced tax revenue cities would be receiving from the state.

For the next nine months, Aldredge sat in the city manager's chair, but the "interim" tag would become an albatross while the city conducted a nationwide search. Then, the city found a replacement and hired Jerry Newfarmer, who had been an assistant city manager in Oakland.

In addition, Aldredge continued to teach college courses at night while working as the city's interim city manager.

Presiding over and making the difficult decisions of where to make decisive cuts in the $800 million Fresno budget proved that Aldredge had the technical skills and know-how to be the chief administrator over

---

[21] It officially was named the People's Initiative to Limit Property Taxation. Voters approved it on June 6, 1978. It limited taxation on real property to 1 percent of its cash value.

a large municipality. From his days as a playground intern to the EOC to Human Relations to the Model Cities, his performances proved that.

He also throws in—jokingly but serious just the same—the balancing act he struggled with as a child.

"Overseeing the city's multimillion-dollar budget was easier than arranging my personal agriculture labor budget during my elementary and high school years," Aldredge said. The line items from those years make an impressive ledger: weekly lunch money, insurance and towel fees, baseball and football shoes, school clothes, school yearbook, pencils and paper, an occasional hamburger and milkshake, and 10 percent of his gross earnings for tithes and offerings at church.

*   *   *

His abilities, first as the interim city manager first and then the city's budget officer, may have caused the scales on the eyes of city bureaucrats to fall off. How many of them *knew* blacks were suited only for social-service roles? How many were *convinced* that blacks simply could not play with the power brokers in government or business, for that matter?

Had they been face to face with state Assembly Speaker Willie Brown, the flamboyant wearer of $5,000 suits and $2,000 shoes?

Brown was the state's first black Assembly speaker and later the first black mayor of San Francisco. He could make or break an aspiring politician, block legislation and control votes. Who in the history of California politics had wielded more power than Brown? Jesse Unruh? Artie Samish? Maybe.

Could Brown play with the power brokers? He *was* the power broker.

Aldredge was about to find out.

Fresno Democratic Assemblyman Bruce Bronzan, a political ally of Brown's, made the introductions in Brown's opulent office in the state Capitol. And disappeared, off to an Assembly vote.

There were pressing Fresno issues that Aldredge wanted to present to Brown. The meeting alone was a political coup.

Shaking his hand warmly, Brown said, "Where are you from?"

Apparently caught off guard, Aldredge replied, "Gilmer, Texas." Aldredge knew immediately he had made a blunder.

It went through his mind: "Why didn't I say, I'm the interim city manager for the City of Fresno?"

Brown didn't miss a beat. "Gilmer, Texas? Is that right? I am from around Marshall, Texas." Marshall is 41 miles from Gilmer.

Government issues? What ensued was a homeboy discussion—until Brown glanced at his watch and said he had to catch a flight to Los Angeles and let it drop that he had to escort actress Cecily Tyson to the Academy Award presentations.

Back in Fresno, Aldredge had a whopper of a tale to tell on himself at his weekly staff meeting at City Hall.

"OK, folks, I won't be going up there anymore to represent the City of Fresno because I didn't make much of an inroad with Assembly Speaker Brown as far as government issues of local benefit. Speaker Brown was so smooth that I clumsily introduced myself as being from Gilmer, Texas, rather than the Fresno city manager."

His management team erupted with rib-splitting laughter.

"To this day," Aldredge says, "former City Clerk Jackie Ryle will ask, 'Jim, where are you from?' "

*   *   *

The same self-depreciating humor and modesty served Aldredge well when he lost out to Newfarmer.

Many observers in and around City Hall thought Aldredge was a shoo-in for the job. After all, he had been the city's deputy and assistant city manager over a 14-year span. He had public support, ostensibly the necessary votes of the City Council and no apparent problems with newly elected mayor Dan Whitehurst.

Did Whitehurst do what many bosses do and bring in their people? For certain, he wanted to usher in a new era in Fresno government. Or was Whitehurst merely an elitist? The evidence, Aldredge said, pointed to the latter. Whitehurst was born with a silver spoon in his mouth; Aldredge didn't come into the world with any kind of spoon. Whitehurst was educated in a private school; Aldredge was educated in the schools of west Fresno.

Whitehurst led the charge to get rid of the influential neighborhood councils that were developed when Aldredge led the Model Cities program in southeast and southwest Fresno. The change was directly opposite from Aldredge's populist approach of community involvement and citizen input as a part of government.

Paul Winter, a savvy veteran of politics for more than four decades in the Central Valley, said, "I still don't know to this day why Dan didn't want Jim. I never talked to him about it. It could have just been that he wanted to bring in a new management team."

Winter also said: "Furthermore, a troubling aspect of Jim's not being voted in as city manager was that Jim was the prime candidate of most people, and a city councilman named Joel Crosby, whose election campaign I had run, made a total commitment to back Jim. Then, on the day of the vote, Dan met with him, and I don't know what was said, but Joel went into the Council Chambers and voted with Dan for Jerry Newfarmer, the assistant city manager from Oakland."

Still, Winter said he and many others wondered to themselves and out loud why Aldredge was always passed over despite his outstanding civic achievements and numerous accolades.

Gary Carozza, a Fresno County health director, had worked with Aldredge on city and county projects. He also had been a student in Aldredge's public administration class at the University of San Francisco's Fresno campus.

He saw the irony when Aldredge did not get the job. "He didn't need to get the official vote for city manager because he had been doing that job all along. In fact, it was amusing to me . . . because whenever you needed to get something of importance done at the city, everyone already knew that Jim Aldredge was the one that you could go to."

But why didn't Aldredge get the job?

Carozza said flatly: "Because he was black. I don't know any other way to put it. Fresno had an image problem, and they were trying to grow from being this farm town, and the powers that be didn't want this black man to be the face of the city."

Seven years later, Fresno was still trying to shed its good ol' boy image. By then, a black face would show diversity and more liberal thinking, Carozza said before he died. "As community enlightenment was happening, Jim was hired. He was well-respected and did his job very, very well, which was different from what most people expected.

"First, Jim would always give you an honest answer. Second, if he didn't know, he would find out or tell you where you could find out.

Third, he knew which way the political winds blew and could tell you whether your objective or proposal was feasible or not."

Newfarmer, Winter said, made a top-notch city manager, and, on the occasions that they worked together on issues, he was impressed. However, Winter said he gained even more respect for Aldredge after council members announced their vote for Newfarmer.

"He almost had a smile on his face when he didn't get the job because he was still able to function and be just as influential, and he had Newfarmer's respect, as well as many, many community people."

Newfarmer's respect for Aldredge was apparently one of convenience. He excluded Aldredge from certain meetings with the mayor and city staff members. Aldredge's No. 2 position in city government still allowed him to serve Fresno's needy behind the scenes.

*   *   *

In 1982, Newfarmer resigned as city manager and took the equivalent job in Cincinnati, Ohio.

For Aldredge, there was more political gamesmanship coming. He again was named interim city manager and held the job for about nine months while the city did another nationwide search. Aldredge was 44 when the council appointed Bob Christofferson as the new city manager in 1983. Christofferson had held the same position in Salinas.

Although Aldredge did not apply for the job this time, the council thoughtfully put his name in the running because of his past service.

*   *   *

The City Council was watching Christofferson closely and, obviously not satisfied, fired him in mid-1985.

For the third time, Aldredge became the interim city manager in Fresno while the City Council went through the legal motions of another nationwide search. The search this time took 10 months.

There were only a few black city administrators in America in the mid-1980s, especially in cities like Fresno where the black population was less than 15 percent. Would he be rewarded at last?

"Having a nationwide search for city manager was necessary to keep the hiring process beyond reproach," said Karen Humphrey, Fresno's mayor at the time. "But I knew that Jim was the most qualified."

Humphrey, Fresno's first female mayor, said, "Jim's performance as a deputy and assistant city manager made it very clear that he had the capacity to be a city manager. But I was also aware that that was a time and an era when there weren't many black city managers around. And Jim was certainly in an era where he had to prove himself, and I responded to that.

"Jim and I were in the same boat because we were opening doors. We were breaking barriers that people had erected. And I will venture to say that there is no question that in this society it is more challenging to be African-American than it is to be female. I think he related pretty well to the aspirations of women and other minorities in trying to get their foot in the door."

After the city's nationwide search, Dr. James Earl Aldredge, at age 47, was named the first African-American city manager Fresno's history in 1986.

"However," Aldredge said, "success is not in description; it's what you do. You've got doers and describers, and I pride myself as a doer."[22]

Carozza said Aldredge delivered municipal services to minorities, the poor and needy, and disadvantaged people in a timely, efficient and unbiased manner.

With equal impartiality, Aldredge gave himself an even-handed grade as a well-educated, competent and professional administrator. "It's a matter of fact that I can compete with anybody doing top-level administration." He never considered himself a black city manager, but a city manager who happened to be black. He never needed an affirmative-action program to succeed.

"When you scream inequality, there's not a whole bunch of folks listening. You can be angry about it, you can scream and holler about it, but that's usually all you can do about it. So, I say, Why don't you just go ahead and be as good or better than the next person, recognizing that you have to. Because if you don't understand that fact of life at this point

---

[22]   A list of organizations with which he has served is in Appendix A at the end of this book.

in time, you can be left at the bus stop whining. Just be better . . . not bitter."

He chose to turn his head the other way about race issues, pettiness, temporary setbacks, looking instead to his faith in God and to understand what it takes to achieve success.

*   *   *

That doesn't mean Aldredge isn't as susceptible as everyone else to subtle slights, regardless of how innocent they may seem. One, in particular, caught his ear, and it was burned indelibly into his mental diary, and he has not forgotten it 58 years later.

During one of those classic locker-room pep talks, Edison High's white football coach was goading on his mainly black team, which was going to face a mainly white team. His intensity and emotion were just short of Knute Rockne's "win one for the Gipper."

"I want you guys to play hard! Do not give up! Show character! One of these days you will be asking any one of these guys for a job, and they will remember your character that we did not quit!"

Aldredge said, "I asked myself, 'What about the possibility of some of them working for me?' I further thought to myself, 'If I get a good education and a good job, the tables could be turned.'

"And by the way, I say this with absolutely no malice, but to show you how fate and faith can work. The tables were turned when I became Fresno's city manager, and I had the opportunity to hire two or three members of that opposing football team that one of my Edison coaches was referring to that night back in 1955."

Chapter Twenty-Nine

SOLVING ISSUES AT CITY HALL

Jim Boren has been an observer of the city's political scene since 1969 when he started at The Fresno Bee, and he reflected about the impact Aldredge had on Fresno.

"He was a groundbreaker in almost everything he did. And when he became city manager, it was not a very easy time in the City of Fresno."

Boren, the newspaper's editorial page editor and vice president, recalled that the City Council had just fired Robert Christofferson, the city manager, and Fresno was starting to have growing pains.

"Even though we had a large population, we still did things like a small town. And the organization was really a small town organizational structure where you sort of looked over the cubicle, and you could talk to everybody and get things done.

"But in a relatively short period of time, Fresno government had become a big, complex bureaucracy, and one of the things Jim did at the time was to reorganize the city to be more adaptable to the local environment that was rapidly changing."

Boren praised Aldredge's reorganization because the new structure exemplified his political philosophy. He said Aldredge was concerned with the basics.

"Jim always knew that it wasn't about politics; it's not about getting honor or glory for some politician, or the City Council, or the mayor. He was about being responsive to the community and taxpayers' needs like keeping the city safe with a strong police force, filling in the potholes, making sure the water runs and the garbage gets picked up."

To that end, Aldredge implemented a non-fanfare, legacy program that benefits residents to this day. For example, he directed the city to begin a city-wide trash pickup program twice a year, and residents could discard almost anything, including furniture, appliances and tree limbs, in front of their houses on the curb. City crews would collect the trash.

Aldredge said it's not important who initiated the program but the fact that he and Fresno took pride, and still do, in keeping the city clean, especially in lower-income areas.

Keeping the city clean also became an issue when sanitation workers went on strike. During negotiations to resolve the strike, Aldredge knew how necessary it was to keep hauling away garbage to prevent a health hazard. That's when he put on overalls and drove a garbage truck. He challenged management employees to do the same and made a contest to see which team could collect the most garbage. Aldredge and his cousin, Redevelopment Director Stafford Parker, won the contest.

Dr. Robert Quesada, a former deputy city manager, said the contest worked because Aldredge led by example. "He was home-grown and felt an affinity to look out for, and a duty to serve, the residents of Fresno. The curbside pickup would also fall under that category. And as far as driving a garbage truck during the sanitation workers strike, he told me, 'Bob, they don't always pay you to do things that are easy and that you like. This is city work that has to be done, but this is no love-in.'"

Aldredge was committed to solving problems and remaining above the fray of partisan politics.

Boren said, "Fresno is a much better place because of Jim, because, as one former city manager said, and I think it was Ralph Hanley, Fresno is a political pesthole and there are people snipping at you from all sides. Jim handled that because he is a man of great integrity, and his word is his bond."

"Jim told me," Quesada said, "that being twice as good as the other person was just a reality for any type of success."

* * *

During other contentious labor negotiations after Proposition 13, Aldredge armed himself with "transparency and tangibles" and maintained the peace. He told union members that the city wanted to give them good wages and benefits so they could raise their families and do it well—but they could not bankrupt the city. He said that would hurt everybody.

He explained there were service providers and service recipients, and both groups were included in the budget, which was prepared by him and his staff with information from the City Council and residents—always with flexibility and "never etched in stone." He said of course it was not his budget but that he was charged with the job of being the best steward of city funds.

Aldredge's relationships with the police and fire chiefs and union members were good enough that he was able to develop ethnic minority training programs similar to the one for teacher certification when he ran the Model Cities. He did it quietly but with profound results.

Boren noted that the police and fire departments were constricted in the mid-1980s when integration and advancement for minorities "needed a little pushing in that area."

*   *   *

He also provided equal opportunities for city executives, using the philosophy of hiring from within City Hall and not from without, thereby forgoing expensive nationwide searches for administrative executives. He thought they deserved to be promoted if they met the requirements of the job and showed "hustle marks," or the indications of being good and professional.

Aldredge was relatively successful with every internal appointment, although former City Clerk Dr. Jacqueline Ryle countered: "There were some times when I thought maybe he went a little too far. I'd say, 'Man, I don't think that person has that much talent.' But he would give a person a chance to succeed or either mess himself or herself up."

There also was the "Aldredge Trickle Up Effect." For example, when he would promote an assistant department head to become a department head, the manager below that assistant department head would be expected to move into the assistant's job. If the procedure weren't followed, then there had better be a compelling reason.

He said, "Occasionally people from outside were hired to provide new blood and expertise into the organization."

*   *   *

Don't get the idea that everybody got a free pass from Aldredge.

To the contrary, Quesada said with a visible shudder. "I took a memo/proposal in to Jim to sign one day. He scanned it quickly, looked up from his desk and asked, 'Are you willing to bet your job on it? If I put my name on this document, and it is not right, there will be consequences.'

"Jim asked, 'Have you done all of the completed staff work on what you are proposing here? Have you done your due diligence on what you are proposing?'"

Quesada shuddered again. "I said, 'Come to think of it, there is a thing or two I forgot in the project proposal memo and maybe need to revisit with you. I'll bring it back tomorrow.'"

Aldredge couldn't afford to give any quarter because he certainly received none.

"You don't get paid to always do easy things that you like," he said. "You get paid good money to, in many cases, do things that most residents don't want to do. That's life in local-level government."

*   *   *

He earned his keep, so to speak, with what he calls the two toughest decisions he had to make as city manager.

First came "Black Monday," so labeled by The Fresno Bee and still remembered as a day of infamy. Aldredge fired the public works director. City Hall observers say the director was revered and feared by city staff workers. He audaciously told Aldredge he would work with him once Aldredge was in the job for three or four months.

Second to be booted was the assistant city manager in charge of administrative services. Third was the director of finance.

These three well-publicized removals were related to a large public works project and disbursement of arbitrage interest of federal money and funding sources for the project. They crossed Aldredge's professional "tolerance line" when they presented a faulty report to him and the City Council on the progress of a multi-million-dollar capital improvement project and the financing sources for the job.

Aldredge accepted a corrected report and apologized to the council members, saying the three had made a human error. An hour later, the three told Aldredge they inadvertently failed to calculate part of the financing, some of which was financed from a different trust fund.

The three made the error of mistaking Aldredge's nature of kindness, patience and tolerance for weakness.

First, he told them that it was a fatal flaw for each of them. Second, he would report the last fatal flaw to the Council. A week later, he made the final report to the City Council himself, and told the council that he would be taking action about them. After his investigation into the major flaw, he subsequently gave notice to the three on so called "Black Monday."

The immediate broadside to City Hall morale was salved when employees were told about the mistakes.

Aldredge's public statement was that the three either did not know—or at least should have known—about the financing and construction elements for the completion of the project. In the end, one person chose to retire, and the other two were fired.

Aldredge sighed and said, "All disciplinary actions, especially firings, are tough, but many times they are necessary to maintain organizational integrity."

*   *   *

Aldredge made another tough decision when a flood occurred.

Aldredge was interim city manager and the director of Emergency Services. He was faced with the choice of letting an irrigation ditch overflow, which would flood a major shopping center and adjacent homes, or causing the city sewage treatment plant to explode because of its inability to handle the rush of floodwaters, which would flood some nearby farms and dairies. The untreated water would harm crops in the area.

After the city engineering staff calculated the number of acre-feet of water that would possibly flood the farms, Aldredge decided to flood the farms and farm houses near the sewage treatment plant. He thought putting the shopping center in danger would be unacceptable.

Dairy farmers evacuated their homes and moved cows to higher ground. Aldredge and the sewage treatment staff agreed to let the sewage go through the plant untreated and into the surrounding area, which could have caused a health problem.

He said his decision was based on the fact that the residents of a city want "to flush" when they need to. Thus, he made certain a multi-million-dollar sewage treatment plant for Fresno and Clovis would not be destroyed.

"That was why I consider my strategy to resolve the 100-year flood to be the second toughest decision in my city management career. However, both decisions were lonely because the buck stopped with me, the interim city manager."

In the final analysis, flooding the farmland and dairy was the best decision. There was no major damage to the farms and homes, and the insurance payouts for damage were smaller than originally estimated.

Chapter Thirty

AN EXCITING TIME

Three things you knew about Aldredge if you worked for him: First, he was going to have his early morning jog. Second, he came to work invigorated spiritually, mentally and physically. Third, he considered his bi-weekly meetings with individual council members a highlight of his service to the citizens of Fresno.

During the meetings, he would brief council members on issues, provide suggestions and take direction from them on legislation or governance, or city policy. Subsequently, he would return to the City Council with policies based on their consensus.

But if a council member chose not to meet with him, there was nothing he could do—other than turn to his main confidante in City Hall: City Clerk Dr. Jacqueline Ryle who was appointed by the City Council. They often exchanged information about programs and policies related to the City Council.

Ryle recalled two significant differences about their professional bond. Of course, she is white and a woman.

She said, "I forget what year it was. All the city management team was out at the Airport Piccadilly Hotel for a workshop. At some point, Jim and I wound up chatting on a scheduled break. He jokingly and chauvinistically stated that I was the only woman in the group, and he was the only African-American.

"He cracked, 'Hey, Ryle, you're here to take notes, huh?'

"And I answered, 'Sure, if you'll tidy up the room, and clean the ash trays.'

"We really understood each other during the meetings with a room full of white men. When someone would say something off-hand, I would discreetly look over at him, and he would be looking at me, and we knew what the deal was, which was often chauvinistic."

*   *   *

Ryle also lauded Aldredge's willingness to provide special training for city employees, through the implementation of Quality Circles, which allowed for participation of all levels in a department on concerns and issues facing the departments.

He placed the training program under her direction because of her special training and organization development skills and knowledge, as she was close to earning a Ph.D. degree in those areas.

Ryle described Aldredge's time as city manager as an exciting time.

"He always, wherever he was and in any capacity, had the ability to influence others. And he did influence city employees by consensus and by a considerate dialogue process to the maximum extent possible as differentiated from a top-down approach of, 'I'm going to tell you to do this or that because I am in charge.' Jim was more a facilitator than a boss. Jim's management style was shaped to some degree by his participation in other important organizations in the community."

*   *   *

Aldredge concurs that it was an exciting time, and for the most part, he, and Ryle, too, had fun with people, even the Fresno press. Longtime Fresno Bee City Hall reporter Jerry Bier remembered when Aldredge and Ryle were in training to run a marathon.

It's grueling, to say the least.

Bier didn't especially want to run in it or train for it. But they kept needling him.

"C'mon, Jerry," they prodded. "If we can do it, you can do it."

After much pestering, the challenge was too much, and Bier gave in. And ran and ran. And trained and trained. There was no going back. He was going to run 26 miles and 385 yards, if it killed him.

Come the day of the race, Bier took off and never hit the wall, usually around 18 or 19 miles. After that, you've got it licked.

He finished with aches and pains and soreness everywhere. He wished he had died.

Aldredge? Bier says with mock contempt: "His wife picked him up before the finish line, and he rode across."

Aldredge says he had a perfectly legitimate excuse: "I cramped up."

Chapter Thirty-One

THE TIME HAD COME

In 1989, Aldredge decided he no longer wanted to be in the management of Fresno's government. More important to him, he was going to resign on his own, rather than being asked to leave, as often is the case in municipal management.

A new career awaited him as an associate professor of Social Work Education at California State University, Fresno.

"As an educator," he said, "there were more people to be helped, and it meant a lot for me not to get fired."

Two City Council members had started to openly criticize his leadership and management styles. He knew, eventually, it was time to go, that 25 years was a long time in an organization, and fresh blood was needed.

Ryle commented that city managers have to constantly be engaged with elected officials and try to find a way to communicate with all of them in the same way, at the same level. And often the seven council members don't like each other for any number of reasons, especially political ideologies.

"They'll talk bad about each other. You've got to fight your way through that. Jim had his own plan to deal with the position of city manager in the City of Fresno. It was at Cedar and Shaw at California State University, Fresno.

"That was his personal plan. He knew he was going to be leaving for academia, so there was none of that stuff about how I am going to save my job? How many votes do I have from the council? And all the rest of that stuff was not a consideration for him."

He knew that one of his most vocal council critics, Councilman Craig Scharton, was not going to change because of a conflict they had had years earlier.

Scharton, then a student at Fresno State, was a City of Fresno intern and assigned to the city manager's office. Aldredge told him he could not violate the moral and ethical tenants of city government by running a political campaign against a sitting councilman (Ted C. Wills) out of the city manager's office.

Aldredge was city manager when Scharton was elected to the City Council. Instead of thanking Aldredge for saving his would-be political and public-service careers, Scharton chose to attack him.

Scharton announced he was going to run for mayor and, if he won, he would lead an effort to can Aldredge.

Aldredge said that Scharton's threats did not bother him and that it was time to move to his third career objective—teaching at the university level full time.

Former Councilman Rod Anaforian lamented the negatively charged atmosphere Scharton created and blamed him for hastening Aldredge's decision to resign.

"I was disappointed," he said. "It was one of the saddest days in Fresno city government because he could not be replaced in terms of ability and ethics. You name any kind of plus, and Jim brought it to the table as city manager."

Anaforian also said, "I understood and appreciated his decision, and I understood the circumstances that had evolved politically. I felt that a few, newly elected council members had come in, and they were very cavalier, very self-motivated and self-interest motivated, and that proved to be the case in time. And the collateral damage of their emergence on the scene included us losing, again, the best city manager Fresno has ever had, in my opinion."

*　　*　　*

Dr. Peter Mehas, a former Fresno County superintendent of schools, agreed with Anaforian's assessment of Aldredge.

Mehas said: "I've worked with a lot of city managers, I've worked with a lot of governors and I've worked with a lot of presidents of the United States, first hand. And I have no motive to say this other than the truth: Jim Aldredge could just as well have been a Cabinet member of any of the presidents or any of the governors that I worked with. He is that quality of an individual."

Mehas also said, "Because Jim knows when to use his influence and position, his success rate is very high. Jim does not sit silently. He knows when and where to leverage his power and his position, and that has been his genius. Jim's administrative success had not been the result of a rabbit's foot or a good luck charm around his neck, but rather because he empowered others.

"And I watched him when he was the city manager, and I admired his ability to understand the nature of politics, but yet not be dragged down by politics, and his uncanny ability to handle confrontation but not be confrontational."

Fresno Police Chief Jerry Dyer said, "He was one of my two favorite city managers during the 32 years that I have worked for the Fresno Police Department. He was very professional and knew how to run a city. But what separated him from most was the fact that he knew how to handle people. He treated all people the same and, as a result, was able to walk away from City Hall on his own terms. To this day, I have never heard anyone say a bad word about him."

*   *   *

The usually ever-sunny Karen Humphrey, a former Fresno mayor, had a slightly different view. She said she felt misled by Aldredge when he resigned because she heard about his job at Fresno State. "I asked Jim to confirm it, and he told me that he was indeed leaving, but asked me if I could keep it quiet. I said OK.

"Then another councilman came to me and knew about it, and I knew it was probably going to be leaked to the media that day, so I called Jim in and told him he was going to have to call a press conference and make the announcement."

Humphrey also felt that their relationship had changed for the worse near the end of his tenure, but she emphasized, despite that, "he was a tremendous asset" to her and the City of Fresno as an assistant city manager and city manager.

"Furthermore, Jim was someone who played a major role in helping guide me through the sometimes murky waters of city government from the time I first was elected a city councilwoman in 1981 through my second term as mayor when he resigned."

When Jim told the City Council in a closed session of his plans to leave, he said he would be happy to stay and prepare the 1989-1990 budget, or he would leave immediately, if it were the council's pleasure. The council asked him to stay, and completing the budget took about two months.

After that, Jim moved from public administrator to educator in September 1989.

* * *

Aldredge also helped the city in the search to find his replacement. He worked until August 1989 with the same high standards he always set for himself. "No way," he said, "was I going to conclude my tenure as a lame-duck administrator, short on dedication and enthusiasm."

Robert Quesada said many of the staff members relied on Aldredge's strength, for example, during the cutbacks brought by Proposition 13.

"And he said, 'Hey, I taught you everything I know, so it's time for you to grow up and do your thing.' And when he left, he was gone. But luckily, he taught us enough, and we knew what to do when the next city manager, Michael Bierman, came along in 1990. He was like a finance-accounting kind of guy, and we worked with him. But he was not like Jim Aldredge."

Jim Boren noted, "I'm not sure what the numbers are now. I think 3½ years is supposed to be the average for how long city managers in Fresno last. And they usually don't have an exit strategy like Jim did. Their exit strategy is in a closed-door meeting of the City Council where the council comes out and announces that the city manager is resigning or fired. So it's a tough game."

Aldredge confirmed Boren's number, saying that "the average tenure for a city manager in Fresno was about 36 to 40 months." Aldredge added that his 48 months was a record.

PART SIX

The World of Education

Chapter Thirty-Two

FROM CITY MANAGER TO PROFESSOR

Aldredge never second-guessed his decision to leave the top administrative post in City Hall for the campus of Fresno State. According to the ways his mother taught him, there would be no "ready, fire and then aim" approach. He had thought about it methodically and patiently and prayerfully. He knew choices made in desperation or under duress often are bad choices.

"I had devoted much peaceful time and prayer to my decision to move on to become a professor at California State University, Fresno. The whole element of patience is the key to one's choices and decisions having good results because remember, as the Baptist church members say, 'Just hold out until tomorrow and everything will be all right.'"

After 25 years of pioneer work through municipal government and community involvement, he liked the feel and sound of Dr. James E. Aldredge, professor, California State University, Fresno. Twenty years of part-time teaching at colleges made the move easy.

He was honored to try to convey the grace that he knew he received from God along with a plethora of opportunities to work to improve the region through the School of Social Work Education. He would teach and train undergraduate and graduate professionals to serve the community.

Fresno State Professor Cher Bee Yang is one of those people. When Yang, a Laotian, was an undergraduate student, he aided professors in their classes because he could supervise in the Hmong language. He and Aldredge had a reciprocal and professional working arrangement as student and teacher. He said Aldredge was his mentor and confidant while earning his master's degree. After Yang worked for Child Protective Services in Madera County, he became a counselor with the Central

Valley Regional Center, which serves the mentally disabled in Fresno County.

Yang called Aldredge his role model and his hero.

*   *   *

Aldredge made it a point to dissolve the demarcation line between graduate student and professor, and, while he was officially Dr. Aldredge, colleagues knew him simply as "Jim." He often would tell them, "I am still just Mrs. Aldredge's youngest son."

Of course she taught him practically everything he knew in the first five years of his life. But then, the tables were turned. At age 5, he had his first teaching assignment, and it was the first time he taught anyone anything, at least that he knew of. The classroom was on wheels.

The family was still living in Richmond, and Mr. Aldredge purchased a snazzy 1942 Plymouth. It had a manual transmission with the stick shift on the steering column. While his father knew how to drive a stick shift, his mother certainly didn't. And young Jim sensed, even at that early age, that his father would quickly lose patience with her during driving lessons. Jim always went along to be the buffer between them.

"I remember," Aldredge recalled, "navigating her through the driving process from the back seat, teaching her to put the car in first gear, and how to proceed from first to third gear using the clutch and staying on the right side of the street and making the proper signals to turn."

At that tender age, Aldredge demonstrated what he calls his "God-given" traits of unselfishness, compassion and leadership. He called on them again when he helped his ailing mother and when he began teaching at Fresno State.

"I felt that I could help other people get and capitalize on the type of opportunities that I had lost, through circumstances that were not of my own doing," he said. For those reasons, he chose the School of Social Work Education over public administration and political science. He also wanted a change in scenery from government-related issues.

So he shifted psychological and spiritual gears and thanked God for giving him the opportunity to help so many students achieve their educational dreams the first time around.

Chapter Thirty-Three

TWO EDUCATORS MEET

You know you'd better listen up when your mother calls you by your first name and middle name and they run together as if you had a new name.

"Jamesearl!"

James Earl Aldredge's mother was boss at home, and, when she used both his names, he knew to come running.

If someone else tried it, he might give you the what-for.

And then he became seriously interested in Daisy Rae Ethridge Mims, and she could call him anything she wanted.

* * *

They first met in a geology class at Fresno City College in 1958. They were part of an informal study group that formed after he got an A on an exam and she only a C. So, Aldredge, Daisy Rae and a few others studied together, though he wondered, Why was he in the group? He didn't need help; they did, or so the story went.

By then, he was 19 and a popular guy—even a BMOC[23], the term popular then—he had his baseball signing money and, for the first time in his life, had more than enough to take a girl out for a 25-cent hamburger and a 10-cent cherry Coke.

In his early teen years, it was "no money, no honey." He laughs about it now and says, "Besides, what girl would court a broke guy who wore homemade jackets and whose mother cut his hair?"

---

[23]   A big man on campus.

Still, studying geology was only that, as far as they were concerned. The fact was, Daisy Rae was married, and Aldredge was dating someone else.

So Aldredge was not as glacially slow as the formation of some geological wonders they were studying, though it might seem like it, because 17 years later, he and Daisy Rae—who was divorced by then—went on a coffee date for the first time.

In the meantime, he was consumed with all that studying, earning four degrees, working 10- or 12-hour days at City Hall and running the Minority Teacher Certification program, a part of the Model Cities program that Aldredge directed in 1970. Daisy Rae had been graduated from Fresno State College and was one of the teachers in the program. She was trying to obtain her teaching credential but, like other minority students, was getting resistance from the college, trying to overcome the bias against minorities. Certainly Aldredge knew her, but he wasn't interested, not yet anyway.

Years went by, and they worked together as professionals. Then, Aldredge returned from Oxford in the summer of 1976, and suddenly Daisy Rae was available.

"In retrospect," Aldredge said, "after Daisy Rae went through her divorce, it kind of dawned on me that this was a really nice lady, and we kind of talked on a professional educator basis, and it all evolved from there. And one thing I really liked about Daisy, we got along well, and I don't even think she knew too much about my baseball career. I guess we just liked each other a lot."

The Daisy Rae and James Earl union hinged on another important consideration for Aldredge: "The marriage would have never gotten started, and if it did, I suspect it would have fallen apart if Daisy Rae were a drinker or smoker, given my past parental problems with a father that abused alcohol."

*   *   *

Aldredge, who still lived at home, was 38 years old. He will tell you—very firmly—he was not a mama's boy. No, he was a responsible son, just as he was a responsible city manager with all of its pressures and politics. He envisioned taking that same commitment into a marriage someday.

He said, "I had to feel comfortable enough financially to support a family. Not just at the time of my marriage, but for the long-range, foreseeable future." The first love of his life, Mrs. Ida B. Aldredge, taught him to be self-sufficient by the third grade.

Who taught him how to be a man, how to treat women properly? "My mother."

* * *

Daisy Rae understood that Aldredge had a longstanding commitment to take care of his elderly mother, and she intuitively possessed the necessary warmth and genuine willingness to help.

She was a mother herself with three children and knew the importance of family. Two of her children, Lori Denise and Terry, lived at home. An older son, Robea, lived on his own. And there were uncles and aunts and cousins galore.

At the same time, she enjoyed her work as an administrator in the Fresno Unified School District. She was principal of Starr Elementary School in northwest Fresno. As administrators, they were willing to sacrifice for each other. Aldredge knew quite well "I'm not the only one living in this house with a career." For her part, Daisy Rae worked around, and sometimes through, the demands of being an elementary school principal and being part owner of a childcare center with her three sisters.

They settled on "one energized agreement," Aldredge said. "That agreement was related to childrearing, completing homework and discipline, in terms of distractions like television, music and curfews. Daisy Rae would be the lead disciplinarian, and I was the on-call consultant because, as parents, we did not want to send double messages and Catch-22s." Terry was in junior high school and Lori in high school.

So, James Earl Aldredge and Daisy Rae Ethridge Mims—his first real love and best friend—were married on August 2, 1977, in a small ceremony in Fowler, her hometown, before the justice of the peace. The justice's secretary was the witness. A small, simple ceremony was sufficient. There was no need for a reception.

A honeymoon? That was a different story.

* * *

After the wedding, they visited his mother in west Fresno and then embarked on a 20-day trip to Europe and saw Paris, London, Rome, Amsterdam, Frankfurt, Monte Carlo, among other highlights. The honeymoon was just the beginning of their 26 "joyous years," as Aldredge said. "Our honeymoon memories and other such travels lasted until her death on Feb. 4, 2004."

Their honeymoon travel also was just the beginning of their worldwide travel that resembles a world map on a travel agent's wall. They saw more than 20 countries and got a perspective not many ever see—not to mention putting Aldredge's special twist on some—and the perspective nobody wants—being bitten by jungle insects and suffering a life-threatening fever.

"By virtue of travel, I now understood and could also correctly pass on research information to students in my college classes. For example, if the class talked about Red Square, which I previously thought related to Communist Reds, I knew after travelling to Moscow that Red Square is simply red bricks in a large plaza next to the Kremlin.

"Then there was the Rock of Gibraltar, where settlements are around the bottom of it, right on the beach, because the rest of it is a great mountainous area that looks like a rock.

"Daisy and I saw the Holy Land where Jesus walked up the Via Dolorosa to be hung on a cross. One would think that the pathway would be preserved. However, it was just a very narrow commercial street with some stairs leading to the top to a church that today houses the cross and burial area of his death."

On an expedition through Quito, Ecuador, in the Amazon River jungle, Jim was bitten by insects and developed a fever and a temperature of more than 100 degrees. Daisy Rae seldom left his side, and he got well a few days later after intensive medical treatment by the ship's doctor.

* * *

Back in Fresno, they began the basics of a new marriage—hunting for a house. They decided on the most practical solution and began to refurbish one of Aldredge's rentals in the Fresno City College area.

He bought the house when it was owned by his fraternity, Phi Beta Sigma, at Fresno City College, as an investment. He rented it to City College students and players on the Fresno Giants' baseball team. "Bobby

Bonds was one of my tenants," Aldredge said. His mother contributed by doing the yard chores—helped by students and players who took a liking to her. He and Daisy Rae upgraded the old fraternity house by adding a swimming pool and enlarging the master bedroom, among other improvements.

After living there for a while, they moved into a condominium because two of her children had left home and Aldredge had no love of cutting the lawn or digging in flower beds. "I would agree to move anywhere or anyplace as long as I did not have to do yard work because yard work gave me flashbacks of working in the fields."

For the same reason, Aldredge jokingly says has never seen the 1970 film, "Cotton Comes to Harlem." The word "cotton" is enough to give him nightmares.

"Even today, when I play golf, I have not and will not carry my golf bag around the course because it reminds me of a cotton sack strap over my shoulder." He jokes that he looks straight ahead when driving on roads lined by the agricultural fields of the west side. "I would get the heebie-jeebies, if I looked down those long cotton and vineyard rows, and thought of working in the fields."

For him, the condominium was his solution, and the new address decidedly helped Daisy Rae in a different way. The condo was about four blocks from her job at Starr Elementary, although it meant Aldredge had a longer drive to his job downtown at City Hall. "Yet," he said, "I wouldn't have it any other way, regardless if my jogging and work times changed slightly."

*   *   *

While a longer commute drive was a minor imposition, Aldredge refused to turn their world upside down by taking a job in a city bigger than Fresno. Indeed, he turned away overtures from national search firms and inquiries at national city managers meetings about moving to larger cities that were undergoing major demographic shifts. He chose to stay in Fresno, and not because he wanted to be "a big fish in a little pond." He stayed because of Daisy Rae's career.

To be sure, Aldredge had a lot invested in Fresno. It was his home town with a small-town feel and advantages—including Daisy Rae's large, close-knit family and coworkers. "Even today," Aldredge said, "former students, Fresno Unified School District faculty and staff members mention how they loved her as their principal and colleague."

One of her admirers outside of education was the Rev. Jim Parks. He knew her for four decades, beginning in the Minority Teacher Certification where they earned their teaching credentials.

Parks said, "Daisy Rae Aldredge was just an awesome person who reached so many in and out of the classroom with her warmth and sense of duty to help others. And to have those two come together for the last years of her life was great. She always had this smile and this grace about her. But I really believe the happiest years she had in her life were those years that she had with Jim Aldredge."

She and Aldredge were described as an attractive couple, classy, witty, humble educators and do-gooders who worked quietly behind the scenes.

At a different time, Aldredge said this about his wife: "Daisy Rae's countenance and actions were to do everything possible to make sure that, directly and indirectly, everything should be good and comfortable for everybody she came in contact with, especially students." She was, he said, "the Clara Barton, the Red Cross rescuer and champion of the downtrodden."

*   *   *

After nearly 10 years at Starr Elementary School, Daisy Rae was transferred to Martin Luther King Jr. Elementary School in west Fresno. Her assignment was to try to improve the academic performance of students whose ethnicity was decidedly different from that of kids at Starr. King had the African-American and Hispanic children of longtime residents, and a growing enrollment of Southeast Asians who were beginning to populate the area.

Daisy Rae's love and devotion to the children and her profession, as well as her cultural versatility, shined through. She was determined that the students at King knew, in the words of the school's namesake, "they were somebody."

"Daisy Rae tried to instill in the students at King that they could be as good as anybody if they were willing to work hard in school," Aldredge said.

Daisy Rae worked at King for about six years before she retired with a "golden handshake" in 1997.

She continued to work part-time with her sisters Dorothy Mae (her twin) and Lavera, and sister-in-law Barbara Ethridge in the childcare/nursery school business.

Aldredge's stepdaughter, Lori, started to handle Daisy Rae's duties during her junior year in high school, and that gave Daisy more choices and flexibility in retirement. Lori and her husband, Marco Brewer, also administer the weekly food distribution and daily lunch program for two charter schools in west Fresno, including the Cecil C. Hinton Multicultural Community Center, operated by the Dr. James E. Aldredge Foundation.

Chapter Thirty-Four

CARING FOR TWO LOVED ONES

Jim Aldredge had been his mother's caregiver long before she was confined to a wheelchair in 2000. She had had heart problems for most of her life, and the poor circulation in her left leg nearly resulted in amputation at an early age, though that was averted. A year later, she developed sundown syndrome[24] and dementia. She increasingly did not recognize her son.

In 2001, he added another loved one to his caregiver duties. Daisy Rae was diagnosed with multiple myeloma cancer. With blood transfusions, chemotherapy and radiology, a person is given five years to live. Then, she was hit with a double whammy that few people knew about. She was stricken with shingles and the condition's horrible rashes, and needed the application of ointment three times a day.

Perhaps it's not so uncommon, but Aldredge sometimes had to haggle with well-meaning relatives and friends about the appropriate times to visit his mother or Daisy Rae. He was trying to comply with Daisy Rae's wishes or the doctors' strict orders. He understood that those took priority, and he wasn't about to waver. The insensitive relatives and friends said he was just being draconian and ignoring their concerns.

It was a dark time for Aldredge. As he took one day at a time, he invoked this godly principle: "When you are down, the most a person should welcome, or at least not fear, is adversity, because it provides God a chance to demonstrate His grace." He also prayed: "O, Lord, just help me make it through the night."

---

[24] Sundown syndrome causes an elderly person to have horrible expectations that hallucinations, confusion and anxiety will arrive with the setting of the sun.

"Jim was second to none as far as taking care of Rae when she was ill," the Rev. Harry Miller said. "And as far as taking care of his mother, everyone knew that if you wanted to find Jim, all you had to do was go over to his mother's house, both while and after he lived with her. His car would always be out front, or he would be working in her yard or on her house, whatever, time permitting."

"Jim's true character shone brightly in the way that he cared for Daisy Rae and his mother," said Felton Burns, another lifelong friend.

Former co-worker Robert Quesada said he never fully grasped or appreciated the depth of Aldredge's sacrifice until he had to care for his mother. "I said, 'Jim, taking care of a person close to you when they are too sick to care for themselves is really tough.' And he basically said, 'Yes, it's a tough job, but somebody has to do it.' There's another example of how remarkable a guy he is."

During their illnesses, Mrs. Aldredge and Daisy Rae became even closer, showing unconditional sympathy for each other. In 2001, Daisy Rae suggested that his mother come live with them because they had a spare bedroom. Although he appreciated Daisy Rae's unselfishness and concern for his mother, Aldredge did not think the new living arrangement would work. "I knew that when one felt good and the other one did not feel too well that both would wind up feeling bad."

A few months later, his mother's health worsened, and he moved her to a private convalescent home. It was a temporary solution because, unfortunately, the private facility was not licensed by the state. But there was a blessing to that. Aldredge's nephew, Gaylen Aldredge, and his wife, La Shelle, had had a desire to begin a convalescent home, and this was this time to do it. Mrs. Aldredge moved in with his nephew, wife and two teenagers.

"This was a God-sent situation," Aldredge said. "It was where my mother lived until she passed away in November 2002."

* * *

Even before his mother's death, Aldredge knew he had to cut back on something. Visiting hospitals and clinics and being a nurse to two loved ones were draining his energy, if not some hope and optimism. Although he still loved teaching, he realized the classroom had become his fourth love—behind God, Daisy Rae and his mother.

At first, Aldredge thought he could maintain his full-time faculty status. However, more and more, he had to ask fellow instructors to take his classes because Daisy Rae's two-hour-long morning treatments often became all-day sessions when blood transfusions or radiation was needed. When her illness worsened, it was impossible for Aldredge to attend committee meetings at the university. Family and close friends did substitute for him, when practical. Of course, he realized this was a short-term solution. After all, they had their own schedules and businesses to run.

Thus, in 2002, Aldredge decided to change his professorial status at Fresno State to part time through the University Faculty Early Retirement Program.

Chapter Thirty-Five

A Simple Memorial

From the time his wife was diagnosed with cancer until her death three years later, the couple's early morning walks and jogs stopped, along with his golfing. "I did not want to make Daisy Rae feel any worse by my continuing to walk, jog or play golf, because she was unable to do much exercising due to her treatments."

Daisy Rae often asked her husband why he quit jogging and golfing. Giving up jogging was one thing, but golf? She could hardly believe it.

Aldredge loved golf, but he willingly abandoned what he called "18 holes of therapy." It was one sign of their enchanted relationship. When he started playing the game seriously in 1986, Daisy Rae had to agree to sacrifice a block of her time with him. At least until she joined him on the golf course.

*   *   *

Daisy Rae's funeral was held at Family Community Church in Fresno. Her funeral was elegant in its simplicity. In accordance with her wishes, the casket was closed, and the funeral lasted slightly less than 45 minutes.

Daisy's cousin, former local television sports anchorman, Dan Golden, read a brief recount of her life. Her eulogy was read by the pastor, the Rev. Chester McGensy, which ended with the 23rd Psalm.

Aldredge said that the reading of the 23rd Psalm was appropriate because he and Daisy Rae read the Living Bible together from start to finish as part of their church's reading assignment.

The Lord is my Shepherd, I shall not be in want.

He makes me lie down in green pastures, He leads me besides quiet waters,

He restores my soul. He guides me in paths of righteousness for His name's sake.

Even though I walk through the valley of the shadow of death, I will fear no evil, for you are with me; Your rod and Your staff, they comfort me.

You prepare a table before me in the presence of my enemies. You anoint my head with oil; my cup overflows.

Surely goodness and love will follow me all the days of my life, and I will dwell in the house of the LORD forever.

*   *   *

In November 2008, former Fresno Police Chief Max Downs remembered Aldredge telling him: "It was tough losing my best friend. But I am hanging in there."

"Jim was so right," Downs sighed. "Daisy Rae was not only the love of his life. By far, she was Jim's best friend. They did almost everything together. They travelled to conferences whenever their schedules would permit, and she even followed him out to the golf course where Jim often played with her brother, John Ethridge."

*   *   *

The church was special to Daisy Rae and Jim, and they contributed time, money and energy for a new building on 18 acres in Clovis.

Aldredge utilized his vast experience in planning and development to assist in the design, zoning and construction of the church. Also, from his tithes and offerings to Family Community, he set up a personal three-year plan that financed a much-needed baptistery. Until the completion of the pool, Family Community had to conduct baptisms at a nearby church.

Chapter Thirty-Six

A NEAR-DEATH EXPERIENCE

Two years after Daisy Rae's death, Aldredge nearly lost his life when he was stricken by "two scary, shocking, life-changing episodes that the doctors and I term 'near-death experiences.'"

"Consequently, during both of my severe physical illnesses when death was a distinct possibility, my understanding of prayer response was important for the following reason: If everyone's prayers were answered exactly how and when they wanted with a positive response, then we are in control and not God."

On March 20, 2006, Aldredge was returning from a business trip to Orlando, Fla. When he was getting off the plane in Fresno, his ears were stopped up, so he yawned and opened his mouth as wide as possible. Then his ears "popped," but a pain shot through his right ear.

Aldredge went home feeling good and got a good night's rest. However, the next night, he felt chilly and tired, and he had hot-and-cold flashes and vomited. He took some flu medicine and fell asleep. Nightmarish dreams awoke him, and he got out of bed about 4 a.m. to prepare his lesson plan for his 2 p.m. class at the university. He stood up but had to sit down immediately because he felt weak and dizzy. And he went back to bed.

Later that morning, Jim woke up feeling sick to his stomach and sweating. Not wanting to miss his afternoon class, he asked a close friend, Marlene Brice, to please bring him some orange juice and cooked oatmeal because he was feeling terrible but hungry.

Aldredge then staggered to the front door and unlocked it for her, and went back to bed, waiting for the orange juice and oatmeal. In about 25 minutes, Marlene arrived. He tried to eat some of the oatmeal but could manage only drinking a half glass of orange juice.

Marlene had to leave for work, and he said he thought he would be all right and, after a nap, would be able to go to his 2 p.m. class. He asked her to call him at 11 a.m. so he could have time to make final adjustments in his lesson plan.

At 11 a.m., Marlene called him. No answer. At 11:30, she called again. No answer. At 11:45 . . . no answer.

At that point, sensing something was wrong, Marlene raced 30 minutes across town from her job back to Aldredge's condo. She found him in a deep sleep and sweating profusely.

She woke him up and felt his forehead. She immediately declared that he either needed to see a doctor—now—or she was calling 9-1-1.

"Call 9-1-1," he mumbled to Marlene. As she was calling 9-1-1, he flopped back onto the bed and did not remember anything after he said "9-1-1." Paramedics arrived and wheeled him into the ambulance. Within a few minutes, they were on their way to Saint Agnes Medical Center's intensive care unit.

Ten hours later, Aldredge awoke. He recalled, "I saw life support lines and tubes all over my body. Later on in the intensive care room, a neurologist started to check my vital signs, tubes, temperature." Then came the usual questions: "Do you know where you are? Who is the president of the United States? What is your full name?"

He said, "After I was successful in answering the questions correctly, the disease specialist, named Dr. Manthani P. Reddy, diagnosed my illness as viral meningitis. Then Dr. Reddy said, 'You had a close call. If you had gotten here six hours later, we could not have saved you. You would have died in your sleep.' As soon as Dr. Reddy left the intensive care unit, I said a long prayer of thanksgiving for God's grace and thanks for sending Marlene back to my house. Grace that resulted in my being taken to intensive care."

When the neurosurgeon came to examine Jim, he found an infection between the skin and the skull just above the right ear, which created a blob-like bump. He prescribed antibiotics for the ear infection and swelling.

The neurosurgeon said an ear, nose and throat specialist would look at him the next day, and he would come by, too. He advised Aldredge that the bump might have to be operated on if the infection were to spread.

As the neurosurgeon was leaving the room, Aldredge told him that he didn't believe he was going to need such an invasive procedure on his head. He said, "Well, Doc, I don't think I'll need such an operation because I have faith, and I pray a lot. Psalm 145:19 says, '*He fulfills the desires of those who fear Him. He hears their cry and saves them.*' Prayer can supersede medical analysis and probability."

The doctor turned and smiled and said, "OK, we'll see."

Aldredge prayed for about two hours before he fell asleep. The next day when the ear, nose and throat doctor made his visit, he said that the infected ear was doing OK.

The neurosurgeon stopped by later and took out his flashlight to check the ear and the swelling. "Then," Aldredge said, smiling broadly, "the neurosurgeon mumbled, 'I'll be darn. It's 100 percent better than yesterday.'"

After two days and two nights, between doses of medicine, nurses taking blood samples and his temperature, and Aldredge praying, the neurosurgeon returned. He said it would not be necessary to operate.

"See, I told you. I pray a lot," Aldredge said.

*   *   *

Do not be anxious about anything, but in everything, by prayer and petition, with thanksgiving, present your requests to God. And the peace of God, which transcends all understanding, will guard your hearts and your minds in Christ Jesus.
                                                      Philippians 4:6-7

*   *   *

Aldredge was in the intensive care unit for about a week of blood tests, X-rays and frequent monitoring of blood pressure. He finally was moved to a regular room for further treatment and recovery, and watched a parade of nurses and doctors come and go, and experienced a battery of tests, some every hour.

"After all," he said, "medicine is a practice. And that's what they did!"

He said, "One of the worst examinations was the full body MRI, which really tested one's claustrophobic tendencies, as well as your back.

You had to lay still on a hard surface for about an hour as the machine was taking pictures of all parts of your body.

"Before this exam was given, the nurses and the medical staff asked if I could tolerate close quarters. If not, they said they would give me some pills that would help me overcome claustrophobia. I chose not to take anything. So I went into the examination room with my eyes closed, so I would not be able to see this tube they were going to stick me in.

"Ironically, although I have a blind left eye from the baseball accident, some of the workers wondered if I had gone completely blind. I assured them that it was a matter of fear, not eyesight. I was scared, not blind."

After two weeks in the hospital, Aldredge's room looked like a floral shop, full of flowers and plants from well-wishers. He had a constant flow of friends and relatives visiting him daily.

In late April 2007, Aldredge was discharged to the care of a home-health nurse, and where he took antibiotics intravenously for four weeks. The nurse checked his vital signs, and the injections were administered by Marlene Brice, who was in a junior college nursing program 45 years earlier. Although she was uncertified, Aldredge said, "That was quite all right with me. It worked."

Two more weeks of various examinations at the hospital followed, and Aldredge was examined by the neurosurgeon, who warned him of the possibility of a mild case of vertigo, which proved to be true. Aldredge takes motion-sickness pills to deal with occasional balance problems.

Despite losing his wife and coming close to death himself, Aldredge's faith in prayer remained unshaken and nonnegotiable. He said, "Faith is in my control. However, grace is in God's control."

As if Aldredge needed another test to reinforce his faith, one was coming. It would be helpful in his personal ministry.

Chapter Thirty-Seven

ANOTHER NEAR-FATAL INCIDENT—
OCT. 26, 2007

Suddenly, Aldredge could hardly breathe and his stomach hurt. He wasn't completely surprised. Just the burrito he ate after a round of golf that afternoon, he figured.

Vomiting or Milk of Magnesia sounded good.

But the indigestion wouldn't go away, and his breathing wasn't getting any better.

He again called Marlene Brice, his friend who was the one-time nursing student.

They sat up almost all night, except when Aldredge stretched out on the couch in an attempt to relieve the indigestion and shortness of breath.

Marlene, recalling the success of antibiotic injections after Jim's meningitis 18 months earlier, suggested that Jim should go to the emergency room at Saint Agnes Medical Center.

"No," he said. "It will go away, and I'm not in any pain."

Marlene said, "But you are very uncomfortable."

Morning came, and she insisted: "Either go to the emergency room or go see your doctor."

By the time they reached Dr. Sukhbir Jahil Manjal's office and got out of the car, Aldredge could hardly walk. He made it into the office, but he could not stand to take his height and weight.

One nurse sat him in a wheelchair and tried to take his blood pressure—there was no pressure. Another nurse tried. No pressure.

The nurses quickly called Dr. Manjal's associate, Dr. Ernest Yamamoto.

He took one look at the blood pressure gauge and said: "Hurry, call the paramedics to take him to intensive care at Saint Agnes."

Paramedics arrived and immediately told Jim a defibrillator was going onto his chest and it was going to kick him very hard. Twice.

"OK," one paramedic said, "he's all right now. Let's go to the intensive care unit at Saint Agnes and hook him up."

The problem this time: arrhythmia (irregular heartbeats) combined with deathly low blood pressure.

For two days, Aldredge rested in the intensive care unit and then in a recovery room to wait for the procedure to implant a pacemaker, in another two days. A full-body scan showed no arterial blockages, confirming his annual physical exam by Dr. Manjal.

Again, a doctor told Aldredge if he had waited five or six hours later, it would have been too late, and he would have died of heart failure and kidney failure.

One kidney specialist, Dr. Amy Gen, said Aldredge's kidneys were damaged but not enough to warrant dialysis. With the right medication, dialysis would not be necessary.

The heart beat problem was addressed by the installation of a pacemaker in a procedure that lasted about 1½ hours and was performed by cardiologist Dr. Rohit Sundrani.

Aldredge was in the hospital for about five days after the operation and was told to let the operation heal for 10 to 12 weeks before he played golf again. At the same time, a physical therapist recommended light exercise.

Aldredge split the difference and was out playing 18 holes in 11 weeks. Wasn't that following the doctor's orders? Not exactly.

"The reality," Aldredge said, "was pure and simple that the doctor spoke plain English when he said to wait 10 to 12 weeks to resume playing golf. So, if anything, due to the severity of my medical circumstances, I should have waited 12 weeks rather than 11 of the prescribed 10- to 12-week window, before taking full swings, especially with the driver." Aldredge thinks he remembers a little sting around the heart when he hit a number of practice balls with a driver and a 3-wood at a driving range.

That little sting was telling him his return to golf was premature.

A follow-up visit to a cardiologist confirmed that. One of the two lead wires to the defibrillator/pacemaker had come loose.

Subsequently, on April 17, 2008, the repair to the defibrillator was made.

Finally convinced, Aldredge wants to avoid a third operation and has tried to limit his golf as only recreational, and has eschewed a cart when walking the course will do.

Then, to add to his health problems, tests confirmed in early February 2009 that he has severe sleep apnea.

Other than these physical conditions and a regimen of eight pills daily for his heart, blood pressure and cholesterol, Aldredge declares he has good health. He laughs and says, "I'm just getting old."

Chapter Thirty-Eight

RETIREMENT AND LAURELS

While Aldredge was hospitalized, some of his coworkers in the Social Work Department took it upon themselves to assign him a class for the fall semester—without consulting him about his schedule and availability. It was an affront to Aldredge the professor and Aldredge the man. Nevertheless, he accepted the assignment and finished his commitments to the university community. Of course the slight was intended to push him closer to retirement, and it did.

Aldredge said, "Both my five-year commitment to the Faculty Early Retirement Program and the department, and to university President Dr. John Welty to chair the University Pointe project [a 45-acre commercial and residential development], until the architectural drawings were finished and the working drawing stage was about to begin, overlapped and concluded about the same time."

After 40 years of teaching part time and full time, Aldredge retired from Fresno State in June 2007. He again considered it a blessing to be able to leave on his own terms, just as he did when he resigned from City Hall.

*   *   *

When Aldredge left Fresno State, the gap he left was as wide as when he left City Hall. City Councilman Rod Anaforian said, "When Jim retired as Fresno's city manager in 1989, there was a competency gap, and Fresno city management was never the same."

Corrine Flores, a colleague in the School of Social Work Education, expressed much the same thing about his departure from Fresno State. "So many of the staffers and the students who were here at the time miss him so much, and we are still hoping to this day that he will let us give him a retirement or even an appreciation party.

"We'll even settle for a social get-together because I think not only his friends and admirers, but also some of his detractors realize what a gem we lost in the Social Work Department the day he retired." (However, Aldredge said he really didn't need a celebration related to his semi-forced departure.)

There was that push, and Florez called it a prevailing negativity that Aldredge was always dealing with. "The negativity stemmed from some of his departmental faculty colleagues. You hate to think this, but it really seemed that other professors in the department would act like so many students wanted to do their master's project with Jim because he would be easier. But I was the co-reader on master's theses chaired by professors in the department, and Jim's standards were as hard as, if not harder, than any of his colleagues'.

"More students in the Social Work Department requested him to be their research thesis chair, and he usually generously gave of himself and carried such an overload because students wanted to be with him. They wanted to be with him because they knew he was the best and that he understood these often first-generation college students from all walks of life who wanted to become social workers in order to help others."

One student said, "Dr. Aldredge's goal was to see you succeed. And he was going to make sure that you did succeed by supporting you, guiding you and motivating you. You could cry on his shoulder because graduate work was not easy, especially if you were working full time and going to graduate school at night. It was not an easy task. However, Dr. Aldredge never compromised being a taskmaster. He was tough. You had to cut the mustard to get his name on the dotted line and their name on the degree certificate.

"And that's why Dr. Aldredge and Ms. Florez had that professional bond in the Social Work Education Department, because they were on the same course for helping all students succeed. That was their goal.

"Because I am going to tell you that there was a period there when I felt some professors . . . it was their goal to make sure that people of color did not succeed.

"And let me tell you, Dr. Aldredge was giving so much more of his time and devotion to students than some other professors for the money. The man was financially well-off. But he told me that he was staying here to make sure students like me made it through to get our master's degrees, and go on and help others."

Aldredge said that it was his encouragement and empowerment of the students that made them achieve simply because "somebody really cared." Thus, their self-esteem and confidence rose. He worked overtime with all ethnic groups in the program. Ethnicity did not matter to him as long as a student was willing to try, try, try and try again.

Florez and Aldredge served on the department's Graduate Admissions Committee for more than 10 years.

*   *   *

Florez said that, when she was a student at Fresno State in the 1980s, there were maybe four or five minority students in a class of 100 in the department. Again, changes were in the offing.

"I can remember that during early admissions presentations over 1991 and 1992, students of color were a small pocket, maybe 20 percent in the department. Today students of color account for over 45 percent of the students in the department. Dr. Aldredge had a strong sense of concern. If he thought a student deserved to get into the program, he would often bang his fist on the table and present an argument that made committee members . . . detractors . . . look like opportunity-deniers instead of opportunity-givers."

Florez said she marveled at Aldredge's complexity. "Jim could go from pounding his fist on the table to keep a worthy applicant from being denied admission to the CSUF Masters of Social Work program, to always being ready to advance or rebut an argument in such simple terms that he would kind of knock down the mysticism of certain elite committee members.

"And I think that probably aggravated some people, because he would just tell it like it was. And he gave many students opportunities and was willing to work overtime and weekends to help all students succeed if they were willing to try."

Dr. Peter Mehas, a member of the California State University Board of Trustees, knew exactly what Florez meant. "Now, this is not to be misinterpreted," Mehas said, "but Jim can be very tough when he has to. It wasn't a chest-thumping toughness, but he was going to stay the course, and no one was going to intimidate him."

Florez added that no one could really challenge him on his expertise because he had successfully managed a dynamic and diverse city, and successfully had guided his students through difficult research projects. In addition, his students did well if they showed him "hustle marks" aimed at helping themselves.

Aldredge admits that he did lose some students along the way, but not many. "Everyone has flaws," he said. "According to my spiritual beliefs, there is only one judgment-passer. I am just an opportunity-giver."

Another link between Aldredge and Florez, the director of the Title 4-E Child Welfare program, was the fact that they used education to forge opportunities to leave grueling, low-paying agricultural jobs they had when they were young. They often teased each other about hot, sweaty work in summer and cold work in winter.

"We knew," Florez said, "that the only way to make it out of the packing sheds and cotton fields was to work twice as hard and be twice as good as the majority. I tried to show others by example, and Dr. Aldredge certainly did."

*   *   *

Another cause for tension between Aldredge and some Social Work Department colleagues could have been grounded in his other achievements and contributions to Fresno State.

University President Dr. John Welty lauded Aldredge's successful efforts in the classroom and in leading the development of the $103 million Save Mart Center.

"Jim made a tremendous contribution to the university," Welty said. "Certainly the students with whom he worked and many of our faculty loved him. He was very highly regarded by all of us for his past work in the city government and the community at-large.

"Jim came to us with some great experience having worked in city government, and I think that he brought a unique set of characteristics to the university. But beyond that, he was a key player in helping us work through the planning of a number of university projects on an assigned basis from the classroom.

"And while at the City of Fresno, Jim also served on the Campus Master Plan Committee for a number of years. He also continued to work with CSUF Association Director Debbie Astone, heading the University Advisory group effort on the construction of the proposed Campus Pointe Project.

"The Campus Pointe Project is a large, $225 million-plus, 45-acre, residential and commercial project to complement the $103 million Save Mart Events Center, and Dr. Aldredge chaired the oversight of each planning element for both projects."

About Save Mart Center, Welty said, "You can imagine there were a lot of different constituents, various stakeholders, who had an interest both in terms of where the Save Mart Center was located, as well as what would be in the building and how it would operate.

"And Jim did a marvelous job of bringing people together from city and county governments, Caltrans, the general community, as well as the university community, and helped us work through all of those issues very well."

At Save Mart Center, the name of Dr. James E. Aldredge is at the top of the commemoration plaque on the wall inside the main entrance. Aldredge also served on the Board of Directors of the CSUF Association and Auxiliary Corporation, which owns Save Mart Center and the proposed Campus Pointe project, for 15 years.

*   *   *

In addition to the Department of Social Work Education, Aldredge worked in the Political Science Department on a buy-out basis for his last five years at Fresno State.

He shifted back to political science when the university's former president, Harold Haak, called him one day and asked whether he would do him a favor. "Of course," Aldredge answered without hesitation. "What can I do for you?"

Aldredge thought the favor might be as simple as giving him a ride to pick up his car or a ride home. Instead, Haak asked Aldredge to finish teaching a graduate class in public administration and policy for him. Haak had a new consulting contract with Armenia to help it reorganize the country's higher education system. Aldredge agreed, and he enjoyed the same success in the new department as he did in Social Work, while also supervising research projects.

*   *   *

Professor Bee Yang, the Laotian, recalled how Aldredge educated him and many of his fellow Southeast Asians about the positive attributes of African-Americans in America. "He represented his race on an educational level. When I come to Fresno State, I see Dr. Aldredge as a black man, and he treats everybody equally. In fact, he treats many people better than many other professors there did.

"When I was getting into the master's program, I started taking a policy class from him. And it was when we learn at school how to advocate for people who cannot advocate for themselves, and he always encouraged the students to do that. And so that is why I said he is my hero. He is my mentor."

Cathi Huerta, who was director of Children and Family Services for Fresno County until she resigned in 2010, is a former master's candidate of Aldredge's. Huerta said, "Even though Dr. Aldredge is no longer at CSUF, he had a profound impact on me and several colleagues in my department who were taught by him in the master's program. He may not be teaching in the classroom, however, the lessons in life that he taught us will remain with me forever. For example, I can remember how he taught me to approach some traumatic things that I was going through professionally at what was then the Fresno County Department of Social Services.

"Dr. Aldredge would say, 'Cathi, in a month from now, is this really going to matter?' And that's good advice because you get so wrapped up in the moment, and you want it for the moment that you really do lose your sense of objectivity. Jim taught us his motto to not be so self-absorbed. He was truly a man of his word."

She added, "He always will be one of the men in my old age, when people say that you can count on one hand the people who have had an influence on my life, he will definitely be on that hand."

Aldredge was named the Distinguished Alumnus for the School of Health and Human Services for his work with students in the department and the community at-large. In addition, Aldredge's meritorious efforts to personally educate students, while encouraging those in and out of his classes to advance their educations as far as possible, resulted in Fresno State awarding him professor emeritus status when he retired in 2007. (Years earlier, Aldredge was named a Distinguished Alumnus at Fresno City College.)

PART SEVEN

A Legacy

Chapter Thirty-Nine

EDISON HONORS ALDREDGE

Edison High School's Hall of Fame is overflowing with athletes who have achieved renown in the Olympics or major league baseball or the National Football League or the National Basketball Association. Though shy of those rarefied levels, it seemed odd that James Aldredge's name was missing from that display case, despite all of his accomplishments right in Edison's back yard. The oversight was rectified at last in 2008—52 years after the last time he swung a bat for the Tigers.

Perhaps Edison finally got around to honoring him because of his commitment to the school's baseball program, specifically, and his dedication to the Edison community, in general.

Nevertheless, baseball coach Cliff Rohl lauded him for his excellence on and off the athletic field, and he said there was no question that Aldredge was one of the greatest baseball players in Edison's history.[25]

When Aldredge rose to make his acceptance speech, he started with a story he loves to tell, especially to people when they first meet him.

Looking out over the crowd from the podium, he smiled and said: "Those of you who think I'm ignoring you to my left, please do not be offended."

Then, he took off his dark glasses and revealed his injured eye, and said he could see out of only one eye.

He injected some humor and drama to try to inspire everyone in the room how a person could achieve a lot in life through God's grace and a strong work ethic, but not by talent alone.

---

[25]   Edison High School was opened in 1906.

Aldredge capped off his brief speech by extolling the virtues of his fellow inductees,[26] many of those in the audience and many other Edison baseball players who had come before and after him. He thanked everyone and sat down to a standing ovation.

*   *   *

"Nothing like that can happen to me." It is a timeless refrain of callow youth—so immortal and indestructible, healthy and strong, hard bodies all—who seemingly can throw a baseball through a brick wall or bang helmets with opponents or out-run the wind all the day long. Until it happens to them.

One day on a Fresno golf course, Aldredge was chatting with future National Football League All-Pro punt returner Clifton Smith. He was Fresno State's most valuable player in the 2007 season.

Aldredge congratulated Smith on being drafted, but he was more interested in knowing whether Smith had earned a degree.

When Smith responded that he still had a couple more classes to take before he graduated, that was Aldredge's cue to make his trademark dramatic move.

He whipped off his dark glasses and gave Smith a good look at his left eye.

"It was interesting," Aldredge recalled. "There was a little bit of shock, and he was taken aback by looking at this messed-up eye. However, my message of getting an education would be less believable if not for my injured eye. So I have tolerated the ugly injured eye in order to say, 'See that, man.'

"And then when the person is taken aback, to be able to say: 'OK, now let's talk in relation to here today, gone tomorrow. It takes a few seconds to be wiped out on a football field or, in my case, a baseball diamond. But no one or nothing can take away your education.'"

He also told Smith to "give it all that you've got on the pro football field, go real hard; but before you leave Fresno State officially, make sure you have a guaranteed extension on your scholarship."

---

26   Ricky Manning, football and baseball, UCLA, Chicago Bears; Jon Asahina, baseball, Fresno City College, Wake Forest University, Florida Marlins, were the other inductees.

A few months later, Aldredge ran into Smith's uncle, James Wright. Smith had told Wright about the conversation, and Wright said he appreciated what Aldredge said. Smith planned to finish the classroom work he needed for a degree.

Then it happened. Smith tore his Achilles tendon the next year, while playing for Tampa Bay, and he missed the 2009 season. Tampa Bay released him before the start of the 2010 regular season when he was unable to return to his All Pro form of 2008. Later, he played for the Miami Dolphins and Cleveland Browns.

"So that's why I don't plan to fix my eye," Aldredge said. "There is an explanatory aspect of just showing what can happen in a split second, but a good education is very good multi-career and multi-year insurance."

*   *   *

Aldredge's retirement also afforded him the peace of mind that could come only from his best efforts to be obedient, to have faith through prayer and receive God's grace. He described that peace of mind. "When obstacles were placed in my path, all I knew was to try, try and try again, while keeping the faith."

*   *   *

Aldredge's teaching in the Political Science Department at Fresno State did not go unnoticed by colleague Dr. David Schecter. When Schecter became the campaign manager and advisor for Ashley Swearingen's run for mayor in 2008, he recommended that Aldredge be a part of her transition team after she was elected.

Aldredge said, "After I accepted the appointment to be on her transition team, David continually said, 'Man, I'm glad you're here to help.' And he's a guy who is really sincere about it. I believe that. And it wasn't a token kind of appointment. In fact, on the transition team were people like Ray Steele, who had just retired as publisher of The Fresno Bee."

Before Swearingen was elected, Aldredge said he met with her, and then with Schecter after the election. "It was clear that, as mayor-elect, she wanted to have someone on her transition team that understood the city government structure.

"I believe that David felt that I understood Fresno as well as anyone. When Fresno's governance structure was a council/city manager form of government, that was the position I held three times on an interim basis, and then, on a permanent basis for four years. Whereas, today the City of Fresno's form of government has changed to what is referred to, or at least I refer to it, as an executive mayor form. It is more commonly known as a strong mayor form of government.

"However, interestingly enough, it's like a soap opera that you watch on television during the week, for, even though I had been gone from City Hall for almost 20 years, the basic issues that we talked about were still the same tune."

Once Swearingen took office, Aldredge became a member of the Mayor's Community Advisory Panel.

Cathi Huerta said she has taken note of the multitude and magnitude of Dr. Aldredge's community endeavors and thinks she knows the reason the mayor asked him to serve.

"I believe," she said, "that Dr. Aldredge shows up in places in which people want to be able to show that they are doing things in the right way. Or that they have gotten the right people involved, whether it's a board or committee or task force, or whatever it is. When you see Dr. Aldredge's name, I think he adds credibility to any endeavor. But I think how he's viewed in this community. He's a rock, and he's credible, and whatever comes out of the effort will be credible."

Aldredge believes that, as a recipient of major portions of God's grace, he must help others wherever he can. And while he doesn't rank the importance of the groups he serves on, he says that the faith-based activities have an edge on the other institutions because they begin meetings with prayer. He considers his involvement as part of his ministry (see Appendix A).

Chapter Forty

THE LEGACY

From the days of the hardscrabble migrant camps and a sharecropper's shanty in west Fresno, Aldredge can look back with pride at how far he has come in nearly 70 years. He is financially set and comfortably retired as a professor emeritus at Fresno State, and he turned 74 on May 1, 2013.

Still, his work day is as busy as ever. There is no sunset in his plans.

As a rollicking laugh starts to build, he says, "I continue to be active in order to take some positive memories to the rest home, but until then, as former New York Yankee catcher Yogi Berra said, 'It ain't over 'til it's over.'"

He is a strident participant on several boards and community task forces to ensure that impoverished residents in west Fresno receive the best educational support services so they are educated in the best surroundings. He tirelessly directs the Dr. James E. Aldredge Foundation, as well as multimillion-dollar, public-private redevelopment efforts with business partners, James Hendricks and Joe Williams, in west Fresno.

HAW '56

The three childhood pals have named their land development group HAW '56, using the initials of their last names and the year they were graduated from Edison High School. Their central focus is to give back to their high school and the community.

Specifically, they are working to stop the brain drain in west Fresno and provide resources, encouragement and tangible hope for youngsters to become assimilated into the mainstream of society and to become leaders there.

Aldredge emphasized that HAW '56 works with Tom Richards and the Pennstar Corporation to provide private-sector funding for a private-public-sector development, which is making enormous strides in west Fresno.

HAW '56's efforts are more than amply evident at the West Fresno Regional Center, which is across the street from Edison High. Students and residents in the area can use all of the center's 40,000 square feet, including an educational and social service complex of 35,000 square feet. Benefits range from children's services to mental health services. The 8,000-square-foot West Fresno Library opened on February 24, 2010, and then-Fresno County librarian, Karen Bosch Cobb, described it as an ultramodern facility that would make the community proud.

The regional center is in Fresno County supervisor Phil Larson's district, and he referred to it as "the one-stop shop."

About the library, Aldredge said, "I am really pleased with the fact that after-school tutoring is available to students as well as all of the technology and computer rooms that, the librarians tell me, adults heavily utilize as well."

Supervisor Larson described James Hendricks, Jim Aldredge and Joe Williams as "three fine gentlemen who bring back so much to west Fresno in that effort."

After graduating from Edison High School in 1956, Jim Hendricks and Joe Williams served in the U.S. Army, and Aldredge signed a professional baseball contract with the Pittsburgh Pirates.

Cecil C. Hinton Multicultural Community Center

In Aldredge's schoolboy days at Fresno Colony, he was too young to know west Fresno was among the nation's poorest communities, but he certainly comprehended it was dirt poor.

The historical Cecil C. Hinton Community Center was about 100 yards away from Edison High School and surrounded by a community needing major rejuvenation and revitalization.

In 2011, Aldredge rented an office at the center in hopes that several organizations with the ability to change the community would become tenants.

In less than a year, he leased the entire center, and it became the headquarters for what he calls the "93706 Renaissance." He knew his legacy would not be complete without him playing the role of a catalyst.

By mid-April 2012, Aldredge, through the auspices of the Dr. James E. Aldredge Foundation, signed a three-year landlord/tenant lease with the Hinton board because the center was in dire financial straits. Hinton center had lost its financial support from the city a year earlier.

As a former city administrator who had built Hinton and several other community centers, Aldredge could clearly see what was happening as Hinton center plunged perilously closer to the conditions of its 93706 surroundings.

He said, "I would be remiss if I became so immersed in my philosophy of being a doer and not a describer as far as the Cecil C. Hinton revitalization, that I did not note the fact that the center's rich history played a significant role in my decision to relocate my Foundation there."

The Cecil C. Hinton Community Center was constructed in 1968 around the corner from Edison High School and funded by a Neighborhood Facilities Grant received from the Department of Housing and Urban Development, with the City of Fresno and local labor unions providing the required matching funds and in-kind labor.

In 1968, members of the board of directors thought that it was fitting to name the center after Hinton because of his outstanding community service as club director of the B Street Community Center, which served youths and adults with social and community services directly after World War II.

The Aldredge Foundation lengthened the center's name, with the addition of "multicultural" and "community," and it is officially Cecil C. Hinton Multicultural Community Center.

The Foundation has also expanded the days of operation to Saturdays and Sundays to accommodate such special events as *Juneteenth*[27], weddings and educational workshops. The multicultural addition to the center's name reflects a change in the ethnic makeup of the area.

---

[27] June 19, an African-American holiday commemorating the date in 1865 when many slaves in Texas at last learned they had been freed by the Emancipation Proclamation (January 1, 1863).

Aldredge said, "As far back as 2008, a profile of nearby Martin Luther King Junior Elementary School where Daisy Rae was once the principal, showed that Hispanics made up 60 percent of the student population, Asians 13.4 percent, whites 13.9 percent and blacks 10.7 percent. So, despite the categorization by some of impoverished west Fresno as a black neighborhood, the 93706 ZIP code area is as multicultural as it gets."

He had received several significant commitments from organizations that wanted to either rent space, originate or relocate to Cecil C. Hinton Multicultural Community Center or utilize the neighborhood park next to the center, which will also be under the purview of the Aldredge Foundation for the term of the three-year lease due to end in June 2015.

THE DR. JAMES E. ALDREDGE FOUNDATION

On February 27, 2012, Fresno Unified School District Superintendent Dr. Michael Hanson announced the names of community members, including Aldredge, selected to serve on the district's Graduation Task Force. Three days earlier, Fresno Bee columnist Bill McEwen referred to the task force as "merely a political cover for a district with a shockingly high dropout rate."

According to a Fresno Bee news story on February 27, "The most recent data from the California Department of Education show the district's graduation rate was 66.4 percent and the dropout rate was more than 22 percent in 2009, based on attendance numbers reported by the district. Some community leaders and teachers have reported a dropout rate closer to 50 percent."

Long before his appointment to the Graduation Task Force, Aldredge and his Foundation were immersed financially in at least a dozen multifaceted initiatives that were producing tangible methods to combat dropout rates. The Foundation was committed to identifying the keys for the permanent sustainability of programs and methods.

Aldredge is adamantly passionate that the Aldredge Foundation has the ability to perpetuate the social program and fiscal sustainability so much that he has bequeathed to this namesake Foundation a large majority of his seven-figure last will and testament.

After Aldredge was appointed to the Graduation Task Force, he said, "The Fresno Unified School District dropout problem is at an epidemic stage that is instrumental in the rise in the illiteracy-driven, dumbing-down of Fresno's collective mindset. The rising dropout problem also is one of the primary fuels for the skyrocketing rise in Fresno's crime, drug abuse and infants born out of wedlock rates. So, I hope and pray with all my heart that the vast majority of this task force will do as well as described."

*   *   *

The Dr. James E. Aldredge Foundation was not established on a whim or meant to engage describers rather than doers. By age 70, Aldredge had long contributed to charities ranging from Children's Hospital Central California to the March of Dimes to the United Negro College Fund.

On January 21, 2009, Aldredge's founding and funding of the Foundation came to fruition during a meeting of the West Fresno School District. He sought, along with district officials, to initiate educational and motivational programs for pupils from kindergarten through middle school. More parental involvement also was emphasized.

Dolphus Trotter,[28] who was the interim superintendent of the West Fresno School District, presided over that meeting and told how he, Aldredge and other kids in the area could swim only in a swimming hole on Central Avenue.

"With his standard brand of humility," Trotter said, "Jim said that, God willing, he hoped to change that situation one day. And sure enough, when he got into the city manager's office to run the Model Cities program, he got the recreation center and swimming pool built here at Ivy Center."

Aldredge acknowledged the compliment and then immediately steered the topic back to the purpose of the Foundation. "I constantly see the parents coming out to root for Johnny in the cheerleading section during Friday night sport games, but there is no cheerleading section for the child involved in academics."

Through the Aldredge Foundation, he proposed a motivational contribution of $5,000, which school officials could use for gift

---

[28]   Trotter died in 2009.

certificates with which to reward students and parents who become involved in the community.

Aldredge emphasized that his Foundation was "not one of those Tiger Woods million-dollar deals. This is just something that needs to be done as a starting point to help motivate students and parents to achieve student success."

At the district meeting, Armando Ayala, then principal of West Fresno Middle School, captured the significance of the Dr. James E. Aldredge Foundation when he said, "Thank you so much, Dr. Aldredge. Someone is looking out for us, and your Foundation symbolizes that dreams do come true, and your efforts will further buttress the improvement of test scores by students in the district, as well as their grades, because of rewards in the program providing immediate gratification to our families."

The Foundation and the school district began cooperating in the second half of the 2009-2010 school year. Parents who volunteered their time were rewarded with gift certificates purchased from Barnes and Noble, FoodsCo, Pizza Hut, Subway, Wal-Mart and Applebee's.

Some of the other examples of the successful collaboration included students in the Leadership Academy being given shirts from their favorite university once they achieved a certain level in either reading or math. At the end of that first school year, students with high achievements in accelerated reading or math were entered into a drawing for a Wii or laptop. Four students received a Wii and four a laptop.

During the 2009-2010 eighth-grade promotion ceremony, Aldredge Foundation funds were used to supply each student a rose for his or her parent. The grade promotion rate was 95 percent.

The West Fresno School District's success rate for students and parental involvement funded by the Aldredge Foundation was so successful that the district matched the Foundation's $5,000 donation for the 2010-2011 school year.

That year, the West Fresno Middle School featured a Student Rewards initiative that included "Pat on the Back," a schoolwide program designed to promote and reinforce positive student behavior. Successful students earned scrip to the student store and a spring field trip to local colleges and universities.

The collaborative effort also resulted in students being trained to develop and refine necessary skills for peer mediation through team-building courses at Fresno's Boy Scout Island. Among many other endeavors was a California Standardized Testing (CST) boot camp on two Saturdays in April 2011. Additional academic support such as tutoring was provided, and electronic raffle items were supplied to students in attendance.

West Fresno School District trustee Hank Hendrix's words captured what fueled Aldredge's collaborative initiatives for west Fresno.

"Jim," Hendrix said, "had the vision to champion west Fresno in its entirety, not just the area surrounding Edison High School."

It was no coincidence that West Fresno School District, like Edison High School, was a part of Fresno's 93706 ZIP code.

"All communities," Aldredge said, "whether they are geographic communities, identity communities or communities of interest, are a type of social system distinguished by the personal or effective ties that hold their members together."

Subsequently, in order to fill as many gaps as possible in the communities within Fresno's 93706 community, the Aldredge Foundation provided startup, sustenance and future improvement, and advancement funding to a wide breadth of programs. There are notable exceptions such as the Fresno Unified School District's "Men's Alliance" and "Fencepost" programs, which were citywide in scope and student representation, participation and the realization of personal goals.

The Aldredge Foundation's collaborations with FUSD began when the district's mentor-director, Darrin Person, approached Aldredge after a Youth for Christ luncheon about getting a few pointers that would improve his mentoring program. Person was a student of Aldredge's in the Fresno State University Graduate School of Social Work.

The Men's Alliance targeted students at Edison High School, Hoover High School in northeast Fresno and Sunnyside High School in southeast Fresno. Twenty students at each school who had two or more suspensions, poor academic performance or attendance, or all three, and were not participating in any on-campus activities were selected.

Most Men's Alliance enrollees were African-American and Hispanic students. However, the program was open to any student who met the rather dubious qualifications. There were also Southeast Asian and Caucasian students enrolled.

Aldredge and the Foundation board liked the fact that the Men's Alliance featured "life skills" classes at each high school where students received credits toward graduation.

During the 2010-2011 school year, the Aldredge Foundation donated $2,500 to the Men's Alliance. The Men's Alliance is Fresno Unified's most successful program in combating truancy, expulsion and dropout rates. The donation was used to facilitate education/motivation tailgate parties at a McDonald's restaurant across the street from Fresno State.

While the Men's Alliance students from the three high schools enjoyed food and fellowship, they were told clearly by Aldredge Foundation representatives that the purpose of the tailgating was to let them take a positive pause between their trip from a high school campus to a university campus and recognize that achieving a higher education degree is the key to their success. Of course, they heard Aldredge's familiar theme: "Once you have that college degree, what you do with it is up to you, but no one can take it away from you."

In a different interview, Aldredge said much of the same message this way:

"You must keep in mind that, while education is the ticket to get where you want to go, once you get a job that hopefully you enjoy, you still need to have the strongest work ethic possible. That way, your total educational experience will truly be a means to an end and not the end in itself."

The Aldredge Foundation also collaborated with Fresno Unified's Fencepost Summer Employment Project, a part of the district's Prevention and Intervention Division. Ten students who were dropouts and who were considered incorrigible were placed in summer jobs in 2011. All 10 successfully completed the summer program.

At the end of 2011, for the Men's Alliance Awards Banquet, the Aldredge Foundation paid for award plaques for Edison High School students, provided $30 gift cards at Borders bookstore for parents or legal guardians of students. Aldredge made a point of commending parents for initial motivation and for making the program a success.

Superintendent Hanson was so moved by the entire program that he expanded the Men's Alliance program in 2012 to Fresno High, Hoover and Sunnyside, and added the Women's Alliance program at Edison and Fresno High.

In May 2011, Edison High School Principal Brian Wall, asked whether Aldredge would consider thinking of a way to mobilize the 93706 west Fresno community to give more personal and financial support to the school. That night before he left the parking lot, Aldredge looked up at the Edison tiger mascot sign in front of the school and went back into Wall's office.

Once inside, Aldredge suggested to Wall that the school have an all-encompassing high school reunion that would be more of a community celebration of Edison High School's rich past and present. A Tiger Town celebration would bode well for Edison's academic, extracurricular and athletic success.

"A Tiger Town reunion-turned-celebration," he said, "where all Edison students, teachers and staff from the school's first day in 1906 until now would be honored along with alumni from Edison's nearby 93706 sister school, Washington Union High School and the general Edison community as well."

A Tiger Town Celebration Committee was formed in August 2012, and it was led by Wall, longtime Edison booster Martha Taylor and Lori Brewer, a successful businesswoman and Aldredge's stepdaughter. Aldredge then was happy to slip into the background of the event as much as possible.

Yet, when asked, he continued to lead the effort in any way he could, whether it was handing out Tiger Town Celebration leaflets at sports functions or using Aldredge Foundation funds to underwrite some of the celebration's costs.

On August 25, 2012, the Tiger Town Celebration was held at the Ernest Valdez Convention Center in downtown Fresno. Valdez was a member of Edison High School's Class of 1957. All Tiger Town Celebration proceeds, minus the cost of overhead, such as the rent of the Valdez Convention Center, went to Edison High School academics, activities and athletics.

Aldredge, through his Foundation, also was making sizable donations to the Edison boys' and girls' basketball programs—with the stipulation that the funding request be for a strictly academic nature such as the Girls' Basketball Leadership Retreat at Fresno State. Or, in the case of athletics, the money could be used to increase the number of Edison High Boys' School Basketball Camp scholarships for fourth-graders through sixth-graders.

Then, there was Aldredge's belief in building self-esteem as another carrot that would improve students' abilities. In October 2011, the Aldredge Foundation awarded $4,000 to the Edison High School boys' basketball program. It amounted to enough money that no boys in the seventh, eighth or ninth grades would be cut from the Edison Computech Junior High or High School ninth-grade basketball teams.

However, as much as Aldredge vigorously supports using the Aldredge Foundation to enhance the probability of student-athlete success, he was absolutely the wrong person to approach about paying for any type of elite basketball traveling squad.

"I told Edison boys' basketball coach, Timothy Wilkins, that I would not fund Edison's traveling squad. The kids who rank No. 1 through 15 on a team will always be taken care of in some form or another. Jim Aldredge's overwhelming focus is not how to help the kids ranked 1 through 15, but the kids ranging from 16 through 150 to succeed in high school."

The Aldredge Foundation also provided modest funding for the Edison High School baseball and softball teams.

Furthermore, at the request of the Edison High School baseball coach, Cliff Rohl, Aldredge participated in a series of organizational and planning meetings, as well as financially through the Foundation to the long awaited and badly needed coordination and merger of Edison High School baseball, Edison Babe Ruth and Little League, and the local branch of the national organization Reviving Baseball to the Inner City (RBI).

The collaboration produced two clinics for Edison baseball players at Chukchansi Park, the home of the San Francisco Giants' Triple A team, the Fresno Grizzlies. Edison players and coaches got the opportunity to learn techniques from some of the area's top coaches, including former Fresno State coach Bob Bennett, a member of college baseball's Hall of Fame.

Baseball and basketball weren't the only sports important to Aldredge.

During the summer of 2011, Aldredge was telling friends that he would like to underwrite a summer track camp for fourth-through-eighth-grade boys and girls who lived in the 93706 ZIP code and in the rest of Fresno County. There would be no charge to campers, and each would receive a T-shirt and water bottle.

A few days later, two other friends were bemoaning that young Fresno children in 93706 did not have enough role models. Aldredge pointedly asked: "How can you say that we do not have enough role models in Fresno, when we have people like our own three-time Olympian and USC and Edison High School graduate Randy Williams, living right here in Fresno? I know he would help with kids if he were asked." Williams won a gold medal in 1972, a silver medal in 1976 and made the 1980 team that did not participate in the Moscow Olympics.

Then Jim thought, "Why not Randy Williams as the instructor of the 93706 Summer Track Camp?"

In early November, Jim met with Williams at a local restaurant and outlined his plans for the Aldredge Foundation to underwrite and start a "Free 93706 Track Camp" at Edison High School, and asked Williams whether he would volunteer his time to be the camp instructor with his own handpicked staff.

Williams agreed—as long as the camp would impress upon the campers that they must apply themselves to the utmost in school and to pursue a worthy career. "He was preaching to the choir about academics," Aldredge said.

Aldredge also agreed with Williams about stressing nutritional values and leadership principles—not merely skills needed as track-and-field competitors.

Over the next six months, the details were worked out between Aldredge, Williams, Edison High School and Fresno Unified officials, Valley agriculture insurance agent Paul O'Neill, Don Martin from Insight Design and Print, and the California Advocate. And on June 14, 2011, the "Free of Charge 93706 Summer Track Camp" had become a reality.

The Aldredge Foundation underwrote the eight-week summer effort that featured Williams and his coaching staff of Ike Jackson and Trish Williams teaching campers about track while emphasizing life skills.

In July 2012, more than 20 "93706ers," participated in the Dr. Martin Luther King Jr. track meet in Lemoore, California. It was sanctioned by USA Track and Field. Team members placed first in a relay for fourth-through-sixth-graders and in a 60-yard dash for eighth-graders.

At the conclusion of the track camp, the Aldredge Foundation sponsored a pizza party, and each camper was given an educational packet for the upcoming start of school. The packets contained rulers, markers, pens, pencils, notebooks, calculators and a letter reminding campers that what they did in the classroom would have far more bearing on the quality of their future than what they did on their respective schools' track or baseball teams or on the softball field.

*　　*　　*

In addition to the Aldredge Foundation, Aldredge is the co-chairman of a subcommittee of a federal program aimed at helping African-Americans and Native Americans emerge successfully from foster care. The program covers Fresno, Humboldt, Los Angeles and Santa Clara counties.

Those two ethnic groups make up a disproportionate percentage of foster children, and Aldredge has met three times with consultants in Washington, D.C., trying to frame a national response to the swelling numbers of African-American and Native American children compared with other ethnic groups in foster care across America.

It's another way that he wants to help people, and he puts a slightly different twist on his humorous look at his legacy: "When they wheel me into the old folks home, I want to be able to say, I always tried to be part of the solution, not the problem."

Until that day, Aldredge simply says that he is a "work in progress" because "God ain't through with me yet. And I have some more kingdom work to do."

Postscript

As you have read, several educators watered the flower in Aldredge's life, and he bloomed. But the ultimate inspiration was his faith in his God who planted him here in the first place.

*   *   *

Despite the humblest of beginnings, Aldredge reached the pinnacle of formal education, he ascended to a lofty position in the fifth-largest city in California and he retired as a professor emeritus in academia. Still, one graduate student wanted the answer that everybody yearns to know:

When did Aldredge know he was a success?

Without hesitation, Aldredge answered, "When I received my Associate of Arts degree from Fresno City College."

*   *   *

How does he want people to remember him?

He was a good guy who tried to help make the community a better place to live for all of its residents, especially the poor and needy.

Appendix A

CIVIC INVOLVEMENT

Before and after being named city manager, Aldredge's knowledge, counsel and commitment were sought by many segments of the Fresno community. When it came to helping improve the lives of others, he said, "Yes." His membership and involvement read like a directory of civic organizations. (* Faith-based groups.)

- Academy for Academic Discussion, 1987-1990.
- Bank of America Scholarship Selection Committee, 1985-1987.
- Big Brother-Big Sisters.
- B'nai B'rith Student-Athlete of Year Scholarship Selection Committee, 1960-2008.
- California Association of Leadership Programs, Board of Directors, 1992-1994.
- California Bowl (football), Board of Directors, 1982-1985.
- California Education Administrative Credential Requirements Advisory Committee, 1982-1984.
- California School of Professional Psychology, professor and Board of Trustee member, 1992-1998.
- California State University Chancellor's Civic Intern Advisory Committee, 1991-1992.
- California United Way, Board of Directors, 1978-1980.
- Christian Businessmen's Committee.*
- Community Organizing Resources to Advance Learning, Board of Directors, 2004-2006.
- Fresno Babe Ruth League and Little League baseball, west Fresno.
- Fresno Business Council Rose Ann Vuich Ethics in Government Award Selection Committee, 1998-2004.

- Fresno City-County Chamber of Commerce Small Business Affairs Committee, 1985-1990.
- Fresno City-County Chamber of Commerce Vision 90 Economic Development and Urban Growth, 1990-1992.
- Fresno County Adult Literacy Council, 1990-1995, chairman, 1992-1995.
- Fresno County Council of Governments Policy Development Committee, 1975-1980.
- Fresno County Drug Abuse Advisory Board, 1975-1980.
- Fresno County Emergency Food and Shelter Program, chairman, 1982-1985.
- Fresno County United Way, Board of Directors, 1965-1980; chairman, 1978-1980.
- Leadership Fresno's first class.
- Fresno-Madera Red Cross, Board of Directors, 2003.
- Fresno Pacific University, Board of Directors, 1996-2013.
- Fresno State University Advisory Committee to President, 1972-1985.
- Fresno State University Association of Auxiliary Services, 1988-2002.
- Fresno State University Leon S. Peters Foundation Leadership Seminar, 1985-1986.
- Fresno State University School of Human Development and Education, 1978-1995.
- Fresno Unified School District Commission on Campus Safety.
- Gemco Annual Scholarship Selection Committee, 1982-1986.
- Kenneth L. Maddy Institute for Public Policy, Executive and Advisory Committees, founding member, 2005-2007.
- Mennonite Brethren, Kingsview Mental Health Systems, 2007-2013.*
- One-by-One Leadership, City Builders Board, chairman, 2000-2004.*
- Poverello House, Board of Directors, 1991-1995.
- Saint Agnes Medical Center, Board of Directors, 1993-1998.
- Sisters of the Holy Cross Health Systems Human Resources Committee, 1996-1998.*
- The Fresno Bee Excellence in Business Award Selection Committee, 2001-2008.

Appendix B

TEAMS AND PROGRAMS FUNDED BY THE
JAMES E. ALDREDGE FOUNDATION

- Edison Babe Ruth League since 1964.
- West Fresno Little League since 1964.

Appendix C

- All North Yosemite League for baseball, as a junior, 1955.
- All North Yosemite League for baseball, as a senior, 1956.
- All North Yosemite League for football, as a junior, 1954.
- All North Yosemite League, first team, for football, as a senior, 1955.
- All Central California, first team, for football, as a senior, 1955.
- American Baseball Congress Little World Series Semifinal All-Tournament, first team, 1956.
- Edison High School's Baseball Hall of Fame, 2008.
- Edison High School's Most Valuable Player in baseball, as a junior, 1955.
- Edison High School's Most Valuable Player in baseball, as a senior, 1956.
- Fresno B'nai B'rith Student-Athlete of the Year award, 1956.
- Fresno City-County All-Star football game, as a senior (he chose not to play), 1956.
- The Fresno Bee, KMJ Radio, KMJ Television All-Star Baseball School team, 1954, 1955, 1956.

Appendix D

EDUCATION, SPECIAL AWARDS AND EXTRA-CURRICULAR ACTIVITIES

- Edison High School, student body president, 1955-56.
- Fresno City College, Student Council Commissioner of Athletics, 1957.
- Fresno City College, Associate of Arts degree, business administration, 1959.
- Fresno State University, Bachelor of Arts degree, 1964.
- Co-host, local weekly television show on community issues, 1967-1971.
- Oxford University, summer study course, 1976.
- Fresno State University, Master's degree, public administration, 1976.
- Golden Gate University, Ph.D., public administration with a specialty in organization development, 1984.
- University of San Francisco, Teacher of the Year, College of Professional Studies, 1986.
- Fresno City College, Distinguished Alumni award, 1988.
- Host, local weekly television show, Crimes' Impact on the Community, 1995-1996.
- Fresno State University, Distinguished Alumni award, School of Health and Human Services, 1996.
- Fresno State University, professor emeritus, School of Social Work Education, 2007.

John, age 6, and Jim Aldredge, age 4.

Jim Aldredge receives an award from Edison High School.

Left: Jim Aldredge, front row, and some of his Edison High baseball teammates in 1954. Coach Mickey Mansini stands at the back right.

Right: Miss Patricia Dunklee was one of the teachers and advisors who helped Jim blossom as a student at Edison High School.

Left: Aldredge was elected the Edison High student body president in his senior year.

Above: Jim Aldredge, left, back row, poses with his
Easton Jr. Legion teammates in 1952.

Left: Jim runs
in the Central
California
Marathon.

Aldredge when he was
about the midway point in
his career at City Hall.

Left: As a
17-year-old rookie,
Jim began his
professional baseball
career with the San
Jose Josox of the
Class C California
League in 1957.
He is sitting in the
front row, second
from the right.

Aldredge was among a Fresno delegation that met with New York City Mayor John V. Lindsay to discuss issues in the riotous 1960s. Lindsay lightened the moment during the serious meeting.

Jim Aldredge meets with counterparts in New York City government about racial tensions.

Aldredge and Fresno city officials discuss the racial and labor issues that characterized the 1960s.

Aldredge and City Clerk Jacqueline Ryle present a City of Fresno employee with an appreciation certificate.

Aldredge with U.S. District Court Judge Robert Oliver at a Saint
Agnes Hospital board meeting.

Fresno television co-hosts Jim Aldredge and Al Geller in 1969.

Above: Aldredge shows
his lighter side in a Fresno
fashion show.

Above: Jim and Daisy Mae with a member of a
North African royal family.

Aldredge and two other Fresnans model for another
Fresno fashion show.

CPSIA information can be obtained at www.ICGtesting.com
Printed in the USA
LVOW06s2349220813

349214LV00001B/9/P